Famous
Haunted Spots

By Deborah L. Davis

PublishAmerica
Baltimore

First printing

ISBN: 1-4241-6395-1
PUBLISHED BY PUBLISHAMERICA, LLLP
www.publishamerica.com
Baltimore

Printed in the United States of America

Dedications

To my husband, Gary, who has stuck with me for thirty years and is the "wind beneath my wings" even with all of his medical problems. He is always there, giving encouragement and praise.

To my son, Ben, who is the light of my life. He has always been there for us and I have no doubt that he always will be.

To my family...Dad, brothers and their families, and Gary's family. They have been there during our lowest times with help and understanding.

To my Mom, who is no longer with us. She was a great influence in my life and will remain forever in my heart.

To my dogs, Oreo and Lucy, who have kept me company during the long hours of writing, by either sitting in my lap or on my shoulder.

And, to God for giving me the courage to go after my dream and the determination and ability to reach it.

Love,
Deb

Acknowledgments

Bob Hurst, Hurst Photography for taking the author's pictures
Wade Webb for cover design and illustration as well as help on images
The Carleton House B & B, Karen and Steve Halbrook, Owners
The Bullock Hotel, Arika Huck, Marketing Director
The 1886 Crescent Hotel & Spa, Bobby Gosnell, Concierge
Willard Library, Greg Hager, Director
The Stanley Hotel, J. Scott Holm, CMP, Director of Sales
Magnolia Mansion, Hollie Vest, Owner
The Myrtles Plantation, Teeta LeBleu Moss, Proprietor
Napa River Inn, Nancy Lochmann, General Manager
C. C. Cohen, Alan Raidt, Owner
Winchester Mystery House, Mike Borg, Group Sales Coordinator
Castle Inn and Creole Gardens, Andrew Craig, Owner
The Dock Street Theatre, Christopher Parham, Owner
Hotel Del Coronado, Christine Donovan
The Whaley House, Dean Glass, Administrative Aide
Winchester Mystery House, Mike Borg, Group Sales Coordinator
Troy Taylor, Author
http://www.prairieghosts.com

Table of Contents

CHAPTER 1
1886 Crescent Hotel & Spa

75 Prospect Ave
Eureka Springs, AR 72632
Phone: 877-9766
concierge@crescent-hotel.com website:
www.crescent-hotel.com

Located atop the highest point in Eureka Springs, Arkansas is the Crescent Hotel. AMERICA'S MOST HAUNTED RESORT HOTEL?
YOU *be the judge...*

THE OWNER SPEAKS OF THE GHOSTS
Words on the Haunts from Mr. Marty Roenigk

The owner of the 1886 Crescent Hotel shares a few words about their long time ethereal guests of the hotel.
The Four Ghosts of the Crescent Hotel

A ghost story was recently submitted about the Crescent Hotel in Eureka Springs, Arkansas. I read this story with interest because my wife and I (Elise & Marty Roenigk) purchased the legendary Crescent Hotel, along with the other large National Register hotel in Eureka Springs, the Basin Park Hotel, early last year. Since the purchase we have learned a lot about the ghosts at the Crescent, and in fact, we have made the hotel more "ghost friendly" in terms of being more than willing to talk about our long time ethereal guests.

I was very surprised by the story on the web site because it suggested ghost that were not friendly—pushing someone down the stairs. We have talked with many people about the ghosts at the Crescent, we have read several books that cover them (one of which is available from the hotel), and even viewed a couple of videotapes that cover "our" ghosts. We have never once heard any report that suggested anything worse than a little mischief on the part of the ghosts.

There are four ghosts that have been well "documented," or at least well reported over an extended period of time, at the Crescent Hotel.

Michael is a workman who died during the construction of the hotel in 1886. His room is number 218, and a lot has gone on there over the years. I'm not sure why that is his room; although one report says that he fell from the roof to that room during construction. He is often seen walking the grounds as well.

There is a nurse who is seen pushing a gurney down the hallways of the second floor. The hotel was a hospital for about four years around 1940. Nobody knows her story.

There is a young woman who reportedly jumped to her death from the roof or upper balcony of the hotel. She was a student. For quite a few years during the 1910-1930 period, the hotel was a school for women during the off-season. Other stories, including the detail of a later sighting, suggest that this young student was actually pushed rather than jumped.

There is a man, in very formal dress and top hat, circa 1890s, who is seen in the lobby from time to time. In addition to these four, there are reports of a group of people seen dining in a corner of the Crystal Dining Room (and being served) at a time when the dining room was closed.

Crescent Hotel Tour
An Eerie Peek into the Hotel's Hallways...
Walk with us through the legendary Crescent Hotel and hear of
its ghostly legends. The hotel was constructed in 1886 and known as
the "Queen of The Ozarks" to the Victorians. In the teens of the 20th
century, it was a fine girl's school offering intriguing tales woven with
history.

Hear of legendary haunts and ongoing investigations being
conducted by our trained staff. The Lady in The Garden, Cancer
Hospital nurses, Michael, and Theodora, are a few of the legends to
whet your appetite of the "guests" that reside at The Crescent.

Follow the dark halls below the hotel into the realm of "Dr."
Norman Baker and his Cancer Cure Hospital where many dreams of
a cure for cancer were never realized.

The long history of the hotel is represented through the ghosts
that still inhabit its halls and walls.

After all, they are no different from us—they are just free from the
physical world.

GHOST STORIES FROM OUR GUESTS AND STAFF

The Woman I Saw...
Jack Moyer, hotel general manager, was having Sunday brunch in
the hotel's Crystal Dining Room with his wife Misty when another
employee joined their table and handed them a recent "ghost
sighting" photograph taken by a hotel guest.

Hotel employees, for the most part, are used to seeing photos of
orbs, shadows or other sometimes-unclear unexplainables but when
Jack handed this particular photo to Misty, she turned white. Still
ashen, she struggled to whisper, "It's her...the woman I saw."
Never Been One to Believe...
Steve Garrison, a cook for the hotel's Crystal Dining Room
restaurant for the past fourteen years recounts, "I've lived here
(Eureka Springs) all my life and I have never been one to believe this
stuff." That all changed on two different mornings in the restaurant's
kitchen.

Morning 1: Garrison was "slicing and dicing" vegetables when he looked up and saw a little boy with "pop bottle" glasses, dressed in very old-looking clothes such as knickers, who was skipping around the kitchen.

Morning 2: When opening that same kitchen early one morning, he flipped on the lights only to see "some or all of the pots and pans flying off their hooks." He was quick to add, "I don't drink on the job. In fact, I don't drink…period."

Late Night Customer

A former gift shop employee vividly remembers a late night "customer" she encountered.

One slow evening, she was leaning gently against the display case, looking downward but not really at anything, when she looked up. There, in the store's doorway into the hotel lobby, stood a man looking out of place in time. He was dressed in a long, black cutaway coat with a tall shirt collar and ascot-like cravat, top hat and his face was adorned with mutton-chop sideburns. His trousers were gray-striped and as she continued to gaze down, his image ended around the middle of the lower leg. It didn't go all the way to the floor even though his image was there. It was very complete and lifelike, not at all wavy or wispy."

She blinked and said, "Whoa!?!" In that instance, he disappeared. She sped into the lobby toward the Crystal Dining Room, then back toward the Governor's Suite, but he was absolutely gone. She never saw him again.

Photos had "Orbs"…

July, 2005

I was a guest for two nights (mid-July, 2005) in this wonderful Victorian hotel. I was not disappointed in the least. You can "feel" the history here. The hotel and the surrounding landscape are beautiful, and the view from the second story balcony of my room was amazing.

The ghost tour was super informative and a lot of fun. Ken & Carroll were great. The photos I took during the ghost tour didn't turn up anything unusual. However, the photos I took in the hotel lobby on the day I arrived and in my room, had "orbs" in them. I was thrilled and have shown everybody I know! I WILL be back. I felt safe and secure in this hotel and totally comfortable, thanks to the Crescent owners and staff.

Knocking at the Door...
June 27, 2005

I have stayed at the magnificent Crescent Hotel many times, and when visiting the Ozarks I will stay no place else. I adore the ambiance and history that surrounds the grand hotel.

When I was fourteen years old, I met a girl whose father drove a tour bus. She came to see me at the hotel and gave me the grand tour, ghost stories, and all.

This was, of course, way before the hotel had the ghost tours. I was, and still am, fascinated. As badly as I wanted to, I did not see anything out of the ordinary.

However, my mother heard a knocking at the door at about 2:30 a.m. that woke her up. When she went to check it out there was nobody there, but once the door shut, it immediately started again. Neither my father nor I heard anything at all.

My last trip to the Crescent was at least twelve years ago and next summer I plan to take my husband and two girls to experience the wonderful hotel. Now I just have to figure out how to explain to my nine-year-old daughter that the place is haunted without freaking her out! I can't wait to be back.

Running Out of the Room...
June 22, 2005

My husband, our two sons, myself, my mom and dad, two sisters and two nieces stayed at your hotel on June 20.

My sister, her two daughters, and my other sister stayed in room 205. They had taken the lampshade off the lamp so they could see better while they were eating and set it on top of the television. About ten minutes later, they came running out of the room telling us that the shade had "jumped" up and spun around and then fell on the floor!

Then that night they said that the phone started ringing about every 30 minutes but nobody was on the line when they answered.

My husband, our two boys, and I stayed in room 210. Our toilet would not stop running so my husband took the back off the toilet and saw that the chain was off. He put the chain back on and the toilet was fine for about an hour, when it started running again.

He took the back off once again to find that the chain was off again so this time he twisted the end so that it wouldn't slip off anymore. We went to bed and the next morning when we woke up, the toilet was running. He looked in the back to find that the chain had been twisted back the other way and it was off. We decided that we'd just leave it alone since someone wanted that chain off so badly.

My mom and dad stayed in 209. Everyone except for my mom and dad went down to walk in the garden. They stayed in their room. When we got outside, we looked up at my mom and dad's window and saw them looking down at us so we started waving to them.

We walked all around the beautiful hotel. Finally, we all went back up to my mom and dad's room to tell them good night and to ask them if they had seen us waving. They told us that they were never looking out the window, so we thought they were just trying to play a trick on us until we looked at their window and saw that it was way too tall for them to have been looking out.

Did You Feel That...?
June 8, 2005

I just wanted to send you a quick note, thanking your ghost tours as it was one of the highlights of our trip. My 14-year-old daughter and I attended your tours the last week in May of this year. We are from Iowa, and stayed in your beautiful state for a week. The rest of our family declined to attend the ghost tours because they do not believe in "such things." After spending some time in Eureka's beautiful hotel, I will tell you that I am a believer...because it happened to me!

We have always been fascinated by the paranormal and came to the tours with an open mind, not expecting anything out of the ordinary, yet welcoming anything that might cross our paths. Secretly hoping we would have something exciting to bring back home with us, as in a story, but just as content by soaking up the beautiful scenery of the hotel and the wonderful people of Arkansas.

We just returned home late last Sunday, and therefore haven't had a chance to get our photographs developed yet...however, on our digital cameras you can see several splashes of light that were not visible to the eye when the pictures were taken. These splashes occur on the second and third floors only. I'm no photography expert; sooooo there could very well be a valid explanation due to the flash of the digital camera or something else that scientifically contributed to the lights we see.

My daughter and I also wanted to share this with you. At the very beginning of the tour, when we were all gathered around the ghost tour office door, you were sharing much education with us regarding our upcoming evening. If one were looking at your office door face on, we were standing at the furthest left one could stand and still hear your presentation. Behind us, was the small set of steps that is in front of the former asylum. The evening weather was very warm and beautiful...no storms, and we remember dressing in sleeveless blouses to accommodate the warm weather

Long story short, as we were standing there, my daughter and I kept feeling a freezing sensation on our arms. We were standing shoulder to shoulder and she constantly felt the ice on her right arm ONLY and at the same time, I felt it on my left arm ONLY.

It did not hurt, however it was very much an attention getter. I would compare it to leaving the warmth of your home and running outside in below freezing weather in only a sleeveless shirt. The cold would come and my daughter and I would look at each other in puzzlement and then the cold would leave as quickly as it came. This happened about four times. There was no breeze and as I looked around, everyone else seemed comfortable and no one else was noticing the freeze.

I didn't want people to think we'd lost it or were making up stories, so that early on we kept it to ourselves. It was only after these cold sensations were felt, that you educated us about someone taking the photograph of a being, sitting on the steps in the same direction of where our cold came from. Then you explained to us that we might feel something, smell, hear, or see something and that it was all right and not to be scared.

I don't know what it was...but I guarantee you, something was there. It was as if something were toying with us...and getting a kick out of my daughter and myself whispering back and forth to each other..."Did you feel that? What is that?" It was very close to "Michael's" room and I'm leaving it all to his playful spirit that he was flirting with two ladies in sleeveless blouses who kept quietly asking him "What is that?" He was a tease and if it's our attention he wanted, he sure got it. Michael, may you someday rest in peace.

In closing, thank you again for your fantastic ghost tours and the education you gave us on the hotel and life itself. It will not be forgotten. We look forward to watching your upcoming event on the Sci-Fi Channel and wish you the best of luck in dealing with whatever is in your home as well. Stay safe.

A Full Figure Standing in the Mirror...
April 16, 2005

I stayed at the Crescent November 2003 and 2004. We stayed in Theadora's room. I went to turn the handle of the closet door and it was as if it was bolt locked. Startled, I jumped back and laughed in a nervous way. That moment we heard the door click, I tried the door again, and it opened with ease. I inspected the door. At one time it did have a lock, but it had been sealed with paint, impossible to lock. On that day it did.

Inspired by our 2003 trip, we booked for the next year, and room 218. This room is known for unexplained activity, so we had to have it. We were dying for something to happen and nothing did, or so we thought.

When we got our photos back we had several orb pictures, but in room 218 we took a picture with a full figure standing in the mirror. The man is totally see-through, much detail, arms, hands, etc. Also, he appeared to be wearing a long-sleeved shirt that had been rolled up at the elbows, and perhaps overalls?

This is one of the most interesting "ghost" pictures I have ever seen, so we sent them to the people who run the ghost tours and hopefully you will soon see them on their site.

By the way, the hotel is great, the staff is great, wonderful piece of history, and I know some of that history has remained behind.

The ghost tours are wonderful and the people connected to them are very nice and the tour is worth every penny. I have taken it three times and will take it again when we return for our November 2005 trip.

The Bath Was Over...
March 16, 2005

We stayed at the Crescent on March 12, in room 310. We had something unexplainable happen and we were wondering if you could ask Boyd (bellhop) and the gentleman in charge of the Ghost Tours to see if that specific thing had happened before. Here is the story:

We were lying in the bathtub relaxing, and I felt a bunch of bubbles under my right armpit. I was lying towards the back of the tub and Mandy was lying towards the front of the tub where the drain is. I asked her if she saw them and she said that she did not.

So, I kind of sat up and after that, the bubbles started again. It wasn't like a bloop, bloop; it was a rapid boil type of bubbling. The second time it bubbled for about six to seven seconds, long enough for Mandy and I to talk about it and watch it happening.

Needless to say, the bath was over. We also heard a muffled metal banging in the room, but that could possibly be explained in a million different ways.

Anyway, I can't say I believe in the paranormal, but it's hard to be a non-believer when things like that are happening right in front of you.

Disclaimer: *I didn't create the bubbles, there were no cracks in the tub, there were no jets because it wasn't a Jacuzzi tub, and there was no visible explanation for the bubbles.*

A Hooded Figure...
January 7, 2005

We stayed at the Crescent for two nights last March 2004 for our honeymoon. The first night I awoke to hear a child crying (there were no children on our floor). We later found out that many years ago a child had fallen on the stairs, just outside our door, and died a few days later.

The morning after the second night, while in the dining room, my husband began making fun of the ghosts. As we paid for breakfast and walked out the French Doors, that were locked open, one of them slammed shut…hitting him in the back.

The dining room was empty that morning, so we were allowed to video tape inside. When we got home and watched the video we noticed that I zoomed into the mirrors (I was unaware at the time that I spent so much time on the mirrors) and as we watched, there are ghostly apparitions. One of a lady with a beautiful hat and another of a man with a slightly crooked smile, who looks like he might be German.

There is also a hooded figure that moves in and out of the mirror, as I was filming. We took about fifteen to sixteen rolls of film during our stay. The pictures were all very clear and very nice. We were disappointed that there was no ghostly activity with our camera, until we got to the last roll of film. In the middle of that last roll were four consecutive very, very blurred pictures. We loved our visit and are looking forward to returning.

Someone Was Watching…

I have to tell you that people who don't believe in ghosts have not been to the Crescent.

It was raining hard the night we drove up there from the Basin Park, so we decided to hang around a bit since the weather wasn't cooperating.

We had taken the little tour train earlier that day and were aware that the place was haunted. We sat outside on the back porch, facing the Christ of the Ozarks Statue, while it was raining lightly. I had a feeling that someone was watching us the whole time.

We went up to the second floor and took some pictures in the hall and the door of room 218. Well, *lo and behold*, we got our pictures back and we have a little light in one of our pictures that resembles the pictures everyone has seen of ghosts. On the second floor, the curtain at the end of the hall was turned back but when we took this picture it was not like that. By the way, the picture we took of the door on room 218 never came out.

Strange Balls of Light...

My husband and I always stay in your hotel. We once stayed in room 223. That night, we became fascinated with a loud banging noise coming from what we now know to be the annex.

We ignored it for a little while and then decided it was time to investigate. We opened our door and walked out into the hallway. We turned the corner and looked down the other side of the hall when we realized that the noise was coming from a spooky, dark entrance.

As we walked down the couple of steps into the annex, the banging got louder. We paused for a moment and I remember whispering to Scott (my husband) who or what would be making all of that noise at this hour, in the dark. We walked further down the hall.

It was difficult to see, so we kind of felt our way around. All we could feel were doors with padlocks on them. Then the banging stopped and we heard footsteps stomping towards us! We ran as fast as we could back up the hall and I was literally screaming my head off because the stomping was right behind me! We ran into our room and quickly shut the door!

We were attracted to the idea of what had happened. We have strange balls of light flying around us on our video camera footage. We love to have people over and show them.

One year we stayed in the Governor's Suite (which as you know has two rooms, a parlor, and little hallway entrance). Our friends slept in the blue room and we chose the pink room.

We awoke to our door opening and closing. Thinking that our friends were trying to pull a stunt, we quickly got out of bed and tiptoed over to the other door that leads into the parlor so that we could catch them in the entrance, messing with our other door. We jumped into the entrance and yelled, "Got ya!" We instantly turned pale and looked at each other as our door continued to open slowly all by itself!

We grabbed our video camera to film, but it stopped. We thought, "Great! No one is going to believe us!" But, when we turned the video camera on and filmed the entrance, we got excited again. The lights in the entrance were flickering and fluttering! You could not see this with your own eyes; you could only see the lights flutter through the camera lens...almost as if it were electrical impulses.

More Than We Bargained For...

My daughter and I stayed a couple of nights at the Crescent Hotel on November 6 and 7, 2003. We had heard the rumors of ghosts but we were unaware of any details.

We did not have any spooky experiences while staying at the hotel, at least that we knew of. I had brought my camera and took a couple of shots of our room, and a few more around town.

Our room, 313, had a door to the balcony and I wanted to have the doorway in the picture so the curtains would be open. A couple of days after we got home I printed the pictures off our computer and got a surprise.

Peering through the middle pane of glass on the door, was a ghostly image. You can very clearly see the eyes and mouth of the specter. We did not stay in the hotel looking for ghosts, we just wanted to experience a little of the history. I think we got more than we bargained for!

My Sister Was Being Tormented...

I took my mother, sister, and niece for a two-night stay in June 2003. We had all day pampering in The New Moon Spa.

My sister was being tormented by some ghost or something that was scaring the life out of her. She would not finish her hydrotherapy bath because of the eerie feeling she was getting in the dark, candle-lit room.

We all went to the dining room to eat breakfast. As we were leaving, the latch in the floor that was holding the door open, came up...then the door slammed hard, right in her face!

She shared a room with my cousin and woke up having the most horrible nightmares, and then she said someone got into bed with her. She thought it was my niece and then soon realized it wasn't! She ran over to my niece's bed and crawled into bed with her.

I was out walking around the grounds just at sunrise, taking pictures. I was down at the bottom of the castle, on the road right in front of the entrance to the Catholic church. I was taking some great pictures and took one of the back of the castle. When I got my film developed there was a flash of light in the third floor suite window. The room right across the hall from where my mother and I were staying!

Pushing Something Down a Hallway...
December 30, 2004

I took the ghost tour on 12/18/04. I took many pictures. When I got them developed, I have one picture of the back of a nurse who appears to be pushing something down a hallway.

I Kept Hearing Noises...
November 12, 2004

My sister, daughter, myself, and a friend stayed at the Crescent in June of 2004. We were very excited about our stay.

The first night was uneventful...but the second night was quite different. I kept hearing noises, someone walking around the room, and the curtains kept swaying back and forth.

I made the comment, "OMG, if there is anyone in here, will ya just do something?" Well, the covers at the end of my bed were suddenly jerked off of my feet. I was so startled I jumped up out of bed, got dressed, and went downstairs where I stayed until almost daylight. I do agree this hotel has many haunts...MANY!!

I had taken the ghost tour a year before and got many orbs in the pictures. I don't know if I will stay there again but it's a distinct possibility. The hotel has a great history...a lot of it still lives there.

Something Touched His Leg...
September 12, 2004

My husband was very skeptical until we went on the historic tour. We stopped at the hotel, got out to look around and my husband went downstairs where the spa is. He went into the restroom where he said he saw a man standing by the sink.

Then, the night of the tour we all went down into what used to be the morgue. He felt what our guide called "Raymond," touch his hair. As he was walking around snapping pictures, he said something touched his leg. I feel there is something there, without a doubt!

The "Spirit" Kept Trying to Shove Him Out of the Bed...
August 26, 2004

My husband John and I spent our honeymoon at the Crescent Hotel twenty-five years ago. Our anniversary was August 18th. We're planning a return trip to your area at the end of October.

You see, we had a ghostly experience while there on our honeymoon. We told our families about it when we got back home and a few months later, my sister-in-law read a newspaper article about the different ghosts that inhabit the Crescent.

We enjoyed our stay there immensely, but John says he doesn't want to spend the night there again. (The "spirit" kept trying to shove him out of the bed one night!)

I fell in love with the Crescent Hotel as a child. My dad heard about it and on one of our many family vacations to the Ozarks, we came to stay there. We came back many times and brought other family members with us as well. It was always my favorite place to go. That's why John and I chose it for our honeymoon.

I've always wanted to see the Ozarks in the fall, just never had the chance with family obligations. So now, in celebration of our silver anniversary we are making the time to come!

The Playful Bathroom Spirit of Room 221...
August 22, 2004

"To stay or not to stay," was the question on our minds when we visited the Crescent Hotel on Sunday August 22. We had wanted to see this grand hotel since we moved to Arkansas from California, roughly a year ago.

We, both being history and antique buffs, thought it would be a nice experience to stay at this historical place. We found out that it would be more memorable than we could have ever imagined or planned. No apparitions, orbs in photo's or thumping headboards, no we had to get a ghost or spirit with a sense of humor.

Strange occurrences began happening a couple of weeks prior to our stay. We planned on staying at the Crescent for our anniversary. Valerie had made reservations for the weekend; meanwhile I researched the hotel's history on the Internet. From reading articles on hauntings at the hotel, we ruled out certain rooms that were commonly known to have ghostly activity.

Later, when reading stories regarding the dark days of the hotel with Norman Baker and the victims of his cancer clinic and so called resort; we decided not to stay and Valerie called to cancel the reservations. This is where the strangeness begins.

When my wife called to cancel our reservations, the front desk commented that it had already been canceled. This was strange, because neither one of us had called earlier. We just thought, *"Oh well, guess the ghosts knew that we were not coming."* We joked about it and even told friends and coworkers for a laugh.

You see, we had decided not to stay at the hotel, as we have had ghost experiences prior in California as well as Arkansas. We thought that we wanted to rest and have an enjoyable time on our trip. I don't consider interactions with spirits or ghosts to be very restful. It seems like since they are restless, they like to pass it on to us.

Later in the month, we decided to take a trip to Eureka Springs from our residence in the Bentonville area. We thought we'd stop off first at the Crescent Hotel prior to antique hopping and give it a look and feel. Valerie agreed that if I felt good about the hotel we'd stay the evening.

We walked around a bit and decided to make reservations for the evening, still making sure to avoid rooms 218, 202, 820 and 424, just to be safe. We got room 221, just down the hall from 218 where a worker fell to his death during construction, apparently haunts. We thought it strange to be near this room, but thought that the spirit might be a homebody and keep to his room. Now we think that he might have gotten a little bored and wandered down the hall to our room.

We were too early for check in, so we took a spin around town, came back to the hotel and had a nice dinner in the hotel dinning room. Later, we took photos of the lobby and said haunted areas, hoping to get some ghostly images on the pictures and even joked around about the hauntings. In the room, while jesting about ghosts, Valerie finally got tired and asked me to stop. So I did, as any fine and "smart" husband would do.

Our room, 221, seemed peaceful and had a great view. We watched some television, my wife carefully avoiding the X-Files, and retired for the evening, with the bathroom light on…of course. Valerie had a hard time sleeping, as she does in unfamiliar rooms and later turned off the light. I, like normal, slept like a baby.

We awoke the next morning to the alarm clock as to not miss the breakfast. While in the bathroom, she asked me if I had done something to the towels. I peeked around the door from the closet and observed that the two bath towels that were hanging on the rack, had been tied around with the smaller hand towels to form a knot, with a washcloth lying atop both towels.

The bathroom had been noticeably rearranged from the night before, and items had been moved around. In addition, the garbage can that had been just under the sink had been moved inside the tub. Our toothbrushes had been neatly tucked into the towel on the back of the toilet and toothpaste laid beside. My black t-shirt had moved from the edge of the tub to the shower curtain rail, hand towels moved from the sink to the edge of the tub.

We, of course, questioned whether the other had done this and thinking that the other one had played a joke. Neither one of us had, so we laughed and took photos for family to see and realized that the joking the night before might have been done by a ghost or spirit playing a prank on us.

Wow! That really capped off our weekend! Undeniably, these things do happen. Though I have had experiences in the past that most people have never seen, I had never seen a poltergeist haunting like this.

We know what we have seen and will laugh about it for years to come. You may ask if we will spend the night again at the Crescent Hotel. Why, yes of course, but most likely not in the same room as, we have added one more room to our list of rooms not to hang a hat in.

Being a businessman, and thinking of the best interest of the hotel owners, I think that the ghosts should pay for their own keep...no free room and board here.

The staff should train them to launder the towels and clean the toilets too. It's the least they can do since they're just hanging around and annoying the guests. And, no tying the towels in knots! Rather, this should evoke banishment from the premises. Bad ghosty...no dinner!

Is This Photo of the Woman Very Common...?

August 4, 2004

We were at your hotel last weekend for an overnight stay. We had heard the stories, but did not think that we would experience anything unusual.

We had a great time, and really, there was nothing unusual about our stay...until I got home to download my photos. I have the enclosed pictures: The first we counted around twenty-six "orbs" in the photo, this is during the ghost tour that evening.

The second is a picture taken in one of your hallways. I am not sure if this is the second or third floor. No one except my husband and I were even near this camera, and I am not the person in this photo. It was taken at about 1:30 a.m. Maybe you could help me identify her? Is this photo of the woman very common?

There Are Orbs Galore...

August 3, 2004

On July 17th, your hotel provided the most beautiful setting for my passage into being a married woman. We took the ghost tour two nights before and I made the mistake of saying, "Wouldn't it be funny if the spirits were watching us on our big day?" Not only were they watching us, I think some of them wanted to participate.

I got my hair done in the New Moon Spa, and on every picture that was taken of me, there are orbs galore. In one particular picture, there were three good-sized ones right behind where I was sitting. My bridesmaids and I stood on the main staircase right before the ceremony to take a picture. Out of three cameras that were aimed at us, all three pictures show a misty area right above and behind me. I feel that they were happy for us; at least I hope they were.

Everyone kept commenting on how they felt as if someone was watching them, no matter where they were in the hotel...but they never saw anyone.

Be Careful What You Say...
July 20, 2004

Thank you for the wonderful service. My dear friend and I took a little vacation and stayed the night of July 11 in room 213. We thought it would be fun to take the ghost tour after a day of shopping.

When we checked into our room, we were joking about welcoming ghosts everywhere but the bathroom. Within 30 minutes of being in the room, I went to the bathroom to freshen up my make-up before going to the Crystal Dining Room for a fabulous dinner. I heard someone (I thought my friend) tap her fingernails on the door.

I turned around and found my make-up bag moving side to side on the hook on the back of the door. I just thought the tapping on the door caused the movement.

I answered "yes" and Jane didn't reply. I then opened the door and saw her over by her bed and then I asked if she heard that or had knocked on the door. She, of course, replied "No."

I guess by the look on my face, she could see my shock. I eventually told her what had happened as I fought back the tears. We finally laughed it off and then it was her turn to freshen up.

Again, she retreated from the bathroom a bit white. She said, "Tracey, your make-up bag hasn't quit moving the entire time I've been in there." We left the room, not discussing it and even kept quiet about the situation until midway through the ghost tour. Other than many orbs in the digital camera, and Jane smelling cigar smoke in the basement, it was pretty uneventful.

Oh, my make-up bag never moved again, not that night or the next day. I guess you had better be careful what you say when you truly don't want to see something. We're planning on returning for a "girl's weekend" next year. Our husbands have no interest in joining us, or the guests in the rooms. Ha!

A Glowing White Orb...
May 19, 2004

I stayed at the Crescent Hotel on May 12 in room 307. I had heard so much about the hotel and had checked out the website; I wanted to see it for myself.

I did not have any experiences in my room that night. The only strange thing that happened that evening was when I tried to take a picture of the door of room 218, my digital LED was so dark I could barely tell if I even had the door in the frame. But the next day, when I checked back through the photos in memory, the two pictures were clear enough to plainly see.

HOWEVER, when I got home and downloaded all of the photos, I really got a surprise. I have a photo of the right side of the lobby (front desk and hall to the dining room) in broad daylight and there is a glowing white orb floating across the front of the wood column next to the hallway entrance.

I also took a photo of the back of the hotel and when you zoom in on the upstairs dormer windows, there is the image in one of what looks like a man wearing a clerical collar and white vestments. There was nothing visible in the window during the daytime when I took the photo.

Now I have several friends who want to come back to the Crescent Hotel with me! It's definitely a wonderful place to stay, with very friendly staff, great food, and an air of elegance about the place.

A Grumbling Male Voice...
March 24, 2004

Hello! I stayed at the Crescent for the first time last summer, and will be back in April. I was skeptical of the ghost stories, but let me tell you...my friend, her brother, and I walked the grounds late at night to explore and take pictures.

About midnight we were walking down a hallway that I shall leave undisclosed, and noticed a light over the door and heard the distinct sound of tools being dropped on a plywood surface, along with a grumbling male voice. As we reached the door, it stopped. Her brother peaked over the door, but saw nothing. We checked the doorknob but it was not locked. As the door was being opened, I snapped a picture.

There is a large face with a bowler-type hat floating over the person opening the door. It is out of proportion to any person present at the time. I also have a picture of my friend in front of room 218, with a fairly large football-shaped orb present.

We stayed in room 216, and I awoke to the sound of a person in a dress walking through the room very quickly, and the sound of the main door squeaking open and closed. I didn't realize what the noise was until we opened the door to leave for breakfast, and it was exactly the same.

The most amazing was when I attempted to take a picture of room 218 with my lens under the door (large enough gap). The camera lens retracted and then shut off by itself not once, not twice, but TWELVE times! It was 1:00 a.m. and I thought I was doing something wrong or pushing the wrong button, but not twelve times! The history, beauty, charm, and the uncanny events all roll into a very enchanting visit.

I Have Over 37 Orbs...

March 10, 2004

I went to the Crescent hotel on February 14th. I wasn't a guest because I had never been to Eureka Springs before, and didn't know of its history. I, however, did spend most of my time at the Crescent. I was very fascinated by it, and do plan on going back to stay...even if I have to go by myself!

I really enjoy the experience of feeling people from the other side. I did take the ghost tour to spend more time there, and to hear more of the history. I just took random shots of pictures up and down the halls, and in one picture, I have over 37 orbs, in others, I have big bright orbs.

While going to the morgue, we were in that last leg of it, and I felt a tap on my head. (I was one of the last two in line, my boyfriend being the last). We were standing there listening to the story, and he has a bad ear, but out of that ear, he heard "excuse me" and there was no one else behind him, and I didn't hear it.

I never realized what those orbs were but now that I've seen them, and know, I came home and looked through my pictures here. I see so many more orbs in pictures all around.

Man in the Hall...

February 29, 2004

We stayed at your hotel the weekend of February 20th...me, my husband and our two small boys. We had a great time, we neither saw nor heard anything strange while we were there but we do have a few strange pictures.

One we took outside of the backside of the hotel, looks like a face in the upper window. Our video shows a man in the hall standing to the side, but no one was there when we were filming! We were in a parlor suite, room 302. We loved it, and so did the kids.

We did not take the ghost tour because the children are small but we plan on it our next visit. Thanks to everyone.

The "Perfect Honeymoon"...

My new husband and I were looking forward to the "perfect honeymoon" stay at the Crescent Hotel in Eureka Springs, Arkansas over July 3 and 4, 1995.

We arrived unaware of its reputation for being "haunted," and were took up to our room on the third floor. After being there only a few hours, we both felt terribly uncomfortable, as if we were being watched. It became so bad that neither of us wanted to leave the room, even to get ice.

We ignored it with a shrug and a laugh. The next day, as we were going down to dinner, I, in typical enthusiastic bridal fashion trotted down the stairs a full flight ahead of my husband. Perhaps it was only natural that I fell, but I will say that it felt as if I had actually been pushed. I nearly missed breaking my neck, and as it was, my ankle was badly sprained.

Maybe it was only an effect of the terrible pain, but all through dinner (we were the only guests eating in the dining room at the time) I heard music and voices nearby.

I asked around after we left the next morning, and did more research at the library. I talked to a few other people who had experiences of their own. The people of Eureka Springs itself were quite helpful.

Apparently, a doctor and his wife spent their honeymoon there and the man, having second thoughts, pushed his wife down the same set of stairs I fell down. I could have been an accident or merely chance, but the many other stories I have heard seem to imply that something is going on there. And, nothing feels quite like getting pushed!

The Hat

My friends and I stayed in room 202 on March 24 and saw something strange in one of our photographs. A friend took a picture of us sleeping in the morning and there is a peculiar silhouette of a man with a brimmed hat looking over us. It is not a shadow and we can see the side of the man on the pillow. Nobody in the room even brought a hat to the hotel with them!

Note from author: The hotel sent me this picture and it is definitely SPOOKY!

It is stories like these that adequately intrigued the producers of the Sci-Fi Channel's "Ghost Hunters" program to spend nearly a week in the hotel this summer investigating, filming, and discovering stories of their own. Although those individuals involved in the production of the Crescent Hotel episode have taken a pledge of secrecy until the show airs sometimes this fall, all indications are that the show will reveal even more titillating tales of the plethora of precocious poltergeists that have been checking in but never leaving this Historic Hotel of America since 1886.

CRESCENT HOTEL HAUNTED PRESS

Tales from beyond the haunted halls…

Visitors and guests to the 1886 Crescent Hotel & Spa are talking about the strange things they saw and heard; the press is talking about them too!

Lots of mysterious photos have been taken at the Crescent. Orbs galore, the image of a woman, a garbage sack with the image of a face in it, a maid with something strange on top of her head, plus many more!

Note from author: The hotel sent me these pictures and I could not believe it!

October at The Crescent: More Ghostly Than Ever

The results are in and they are ghostly. The month of October for the 1886 Crescent Hotel and Spa, located here on the historic loop at 75 Prospect Avenue, proved most successful in the area of the paranormal.

The month began with guests checking into both The Crescent and the 1905 Basin Park Hotel as part of the "Paranormal Pair o' Nights" promotion where guests enjoyed a one-night stay in each hotel. Each received a "ghost gift pack" upon registration as well as a list of noted "sightings" for both properties.

"The reaction to this promotion was overwhelming," said Jack Moyer, general manager at both hotels. "We thought we had a ghost appeal but when we sold nearly 100 ghost packages in one month this fact was truly confirmed."

"With the interest in our paranormal side of life at The Crescent, we thought we would make it easy for interested parties to find out more about those guests who checked out but never left the hotel," Moyer said. "Our national exposure on NBC's Today Show, The Travel Channel, and The Arts & Entertainment Network increased the interest exponentially."

Then the big explosion of interest came on October 19 when on the Sci-Fi Channel a program called Ghost Hunters featured this quaint, Ozark, Historic Hotel of America. A show known for debunking claims of ghosts actually captured on thermal imagery, videotape an apparition in what used to be the morgue when "Dr." Norman Baker operated the hotel as a cancer hospital.

"The TAPS (The Atlantic Paranormal Society) team, who videotaped the program in June of this year, was excited, aghast and overwhelmed by their discovery," Moyer added, "and we were pretty happy too. Our phone received a record number of calls, our web sites took a huge volume of hits, and ghost Michael, who I think was the spirit captured, finally could be 'seen' by the world."

TAPS takes mysterious situations and stories like those at the Crescent Hotel and tries to recreate them. It doesn't take ghost tales at face value and doesn't consider people's experiences evidence unless TAPS can capture it on audio or video.

TAPS uses state-of-the-art equipment such as a DVR system, numerous cameras that work best in total darkness, thermal energy cameras to detect temperature changes, air ionizers, remote cameras, and more. Staff members are currently working on a motion detector system using microwaves to ascertain changes in room density.

I repeat though that all of the reports have been at best friendly, at worst mischievous.

Two Web sites represent TAP's ghost hunting efforts.

The Sci-Fi Channel's Ghost Hunters site, www.scifi.com/ghosthunters, contains a mix of humor by combining plumbing elements with information on the "Ghost Hunters" series. The TAPS site is the-atlantic-paranormal-society.com.

SO…if you're looking for a good, spooky place to spend the night, check in at The Crescent Hotel & Spa!!!

CHAPTER 2
The Magnolia Mansion

2127 Prytania Street • New Orleans, LA 70130
Local & International callers dial (504) 412-9500 •
Long Distance dial toll free 888-222-9235
Fax (504) 412-9502 or Email us at info@magnoliamansion.com

Magnolia Mansion is for those seeking an unforgettable experience!
It is for those who want something Magical, Romantic and Peaceful
and not just an overnight stay. The memory of Magnolia Mansion will
haunt you.

New Orleans is one of the oldest cities in the United States and one of the most haunted cities in the world. Come and experience the hauntings of our Crescent City. Why not start off by staying at a Haunted Mansion? Yes, we have our share of friendly resident ghosts at Magnolia Mansion and if you're lucky, you may have a spirited encounter. We won't tell you what to expect, we will let YOU tell us what your experience is. If you would like to have a Haunted happening then make your request known upon entering the Mansion. Be aware, if you don't invite them, they may not make themselves known.

SO, *come on in* but be careful what you wish for,
YOU JUST MIGHT GET IT!
Here are just a few comments to Hollie Vest, the owner, from some guests who had their request fulfilled.
2/4–7/05 - Hey Hollie, have you ever seen anything like this? Roberta and I were walking back from the little collection of stores at the end of your street. We had found some great items to take home with us on Sunday. It was getting late and the bags were heavy with all the things we just bought, so we decided to head back to the house, drop off the bags, and call a cab to go to dinner. While we were waiting out front, I decided to take some pictures of Roberta standing in front of MM. It was about 6:00 PM, the night was clear and there wasn't anyone around us. The first picture was a mistake, the camera just went off in my hands; the second was the intended shot. We've had several professional photographers examine the pictures and the negatives and none can come up with any kind of explanation other than, what you see is in the picture. Whatever was there was captured on those two frames. Creepy AND cool!
Ocala, Florida
Hollie, just a quick note to say "thank you" for your wonderful hospitality. We had a great time and will definitely be back. But we also wanted to share with you something incredible. Today as we were reviewing our pictures of the entry hall, we noticed two orbs in the picture. Since we take digital pictures, we know there is no film flaw nor can we see anything else in the hallway that would make a reflection in the round shape. We are certain they are some of the spirits of the house who have let themselves be known. Since we didn't get a visit from one while we were there (although we still think the cell phone alarm was the spirit having fun with us), maybe they wanted us to know that they really are there. We've attached the photo so you can see for yourself.

Hollie, first of all thank you so much for making our trip to New Orleans so wonderful. I don't know if you remember, but when we came back from the Cemetery Tour with Mary on 12/8/03, Jim took pictures of the Christmas lights that had just been put up at the Mansion that day. In the picture, there are four orbs. I also got a picture of the orb in the cemetery; that was Emily. We also forgot to tell you, that evening when we got back to our room we couldn't get the TV to stay on. It would stay on for about ten minutes then just click off. The next morning, there was no problem whatsoever with the television. Do you think Emily followed us back from the Cemetery?

4/10/05 - Hi, I hope you will add this to your guest book/haunted happenings web page. My husband and I fell in love with the mansion during our stay. **The Napoleon room** was pure decadence in all its blue and golden glory. The entire place was so inviting. On our third sunny afternoon, hubby decided to take a nap while I read a book in the front parlor. As is most afternoons, the mansion was empty…staff hidden away in the back office, other guests out on tours. I felt like we were the only people home. I took my slippers off and got comfortable. After a while of complete silence, I heard footsteps in the hallway. I immediately put my slippers back on in case it was a staffer who might frown upon my bare feet. But no one came along so I took them off again. I had a perfect view of the hallway. To make a long story short, over the course of the next 20 minutes I did this slip on-slip off game as I kept hearing footsteps but never seeing anyone, never hearing any of the very creaky doors open or close, never heard anyone on the stairs or in the lobby or dining room. I stopped reading altogether and watched the hallway for signs of the owner of these footsteps. The steps were very clearly walking from one end of the hall to the other, like a pacing. My ears' sense of depth perception picked up on that quickly. But again, no one ever passed by. After awhile, the steps stopped, but a new sensation arose. The room was warm and still, but the upper portion of my left arm, which I had just rested on the arm of the sofa, became amazingly cold all of a sudden, and the hairs were standing up straight. I'm convinced someone was looking over my shoulder, asking me to keep a more formal attitude and put my slippers back on. Once I put them on and left them on, everything returned to "normal." Thanks again for your hospitality! *Boston, MA*

4/15/05 - This was like a trip back in time. Everything was beautiful. The spirits were with us last night. It was a pleasant visit. We plan to return with our friends from Mississippi.
Poplarville, MS

4/15/05 - What a beautiful mansion! We thoroughly enjoyed our stay here. We even heard ghostly footsteps around 3:00 A.M. We will be back and hope to stay every time we come to New Orleans.
Columbia, TN

We had a very quiet and peaceful stay in your lovely home with only one "incident." This morning I awakened early feeling overheated. Being unable to fall asleep again, I went over to one of the armchairs and began meditating. I fell into a deep relaxation and felt someone gripping tightly onto my right wrist. It seemed to be the hand of a child but the grip was quite strong and I ultimately had to pry off the thin fingers that were wrapped around my wrist. When I opened my eyes, I was rather startled to see no one was there. I went back to bed and dreamed of a young girl who was walking up the street followed a few yards behind by an older gentleman who appeared to be her father. Suddenly, the young girl perhaps around eleven or twelve years of age darted into the street and was hit by a car and killed. I don't know if this was the same child or merely my brain construing an explanation. Thanks for an unusually interesting stay.
Davis, CA

11/5/04 - Thank you so very much! Magnolia Mansion has been the highlight of our visit to New Orleans! Bourbon Street, the iron work in the French Quarter and even the tours seem to pale in comparison to the peaceful tranquility we found here. The room was breathtaking and the tub was sheer pleasure! We saw no ghosts; yet in the wee hours, I heard the soft tinkling notes of a music box. I'm told others have heard it and am now not fearing for my sanity. Thank you, thank you, and thank you for opening up your home to visitors! We shall be back soon. Take care.

Austin, TX
11/1-3/04 - Thank you for a lovely stay. We are in town for Sesame Street Live playing at the UNO center and we had a few days off. The rooms are absolutely gorgeous and so comfortable. Everyone was very welcoming, including the hosts and the ghosts. We had a 5:30 a.m. wake up call from the man on the roof (footsteps) during the storm. In addition, the little girl watching over us in our sleep the night before, visited Jason. We got a little scared, but asked if they would let us be and they were nice enough to move on.

10/30-11/3/04 - It was my first time visiting New Orleans and what a wonderful experience. The rooms are absolutely amazing. And there are spirits all over. One night the glass was turned upside down when I came back to get more water. Footsteps were heard and I saw orbs at Lafayette Cemetery around midnight last night. I love this place and I love New Orleans. Thank you.

10/7/04 - My sister and I stayed in the Mardi Gras room and had a very strange experience. She went up to the room the first night and I stayed in the parlor reading. When I went up to the room, the door was locked. After knocking for near a half hour, I got Hollie to let me in (thinking my sister was sleeping). Upon opening the door, she was sitting on the bed watching TV. She never heard me knocking!

Orenskow, KY
9/5/04 - We are on our honeymoon. Thank you so much for some wonderful memories, we stayed in the Vampire room and watched "Interview with the Vampire." It was really scary!

London
9/4/04 -'Thank you so much for your wonderful hospitality! We especially enjoyed the gorgeous décor and our time in the Mardi Gras room. The ghostly visitors were helpful and not scary at all! We'll be sure to come back the next time were in N'awlins!

Oakland, CA
09/04 - What a great place! If I'm not mistaken "someone," sat on my bed last night (a spirit maybe?)

Waco, TX

7/5/04 - I was enchanted! Thank you for making this experience in New Orleans even better, Hollie I will always remember this big house with the high ceilings...and I'll remember the ghost and the noises above my head.

7/28/04 - We arrived on July 25 and stayed in the Vampire's Lair to celebrate our first night together as a married couple. I had an experience the first night. I wasn't feeling well and during the night had taken the covers off. A little while later, I felt them pulled up on me, tucked around me and my cheek brushed by a cold hand. I looked over at my husband to see if it was him and he was on the far side of the bed with his back to me (sound asleep).

Staying here Hollie has been a wonderful experience (even the ghost) and your warmth and compassion and caring for your guests is indescribable. Thank you so much for the flowers and we will be back to celebrate our anniversary. *Julian, CA*

Jul 1, 03 - Hollie, what a divine pleasure it was to meet you both. Your southern hospitality has convinced us to move here and relocate our business. Tell the ghost gentleman in the Vampire room good-bye for us. Had a wonderful time and you went that extra mile to perfect it. Thank you so very much for being you. *CA*

Apr 1, 03 - A wonderful stay! My friend Beth and I stayed in the Mardi Gras room. The ghosts were very polite and friendly. Overall, a wonderful, wonderful place.

Rockford, IL

3/6/03- Dear Hollie, I love this place, I felt right at home when I came the first time. I just wish I could have slept some, but your ghost residents didn't let me; but I guess I asked for it. When I came in, I mentioned that I would like to hear or see some ghosts and I guess they heard me because they woke me up every five minutes!

3/13/03 We had an absolutely fabulous time in "N'awlins." It was so nice to come back to such a peaceful and beautiful retreat from the French Quarter chaos. The ghosts were entertaining, especially to Heather, who heard the music box twice and footsteps in the hall. The furnishings were spectacular just like in a museum, but we got to sit on them. The staff has been so friendly and extremely helpful. Kristian was the perfect "host," calling all over town for whatever we needed. If there is any way possible to return this will be our destination. **From one innkeeper to another—this was "the best."** *Napa, CA.*

We will always talk of this for years to come and we will always stay with you when we return to New Orleans. Although we didn't hear any footsteps in the night, we can add to the haunted history to say the first two nights we stayed there Danielle and I shared almost identical vivid dreams about vampires. It could have been the red walls and satin sheets, mind you.

Says Patty Gay, president of the Preservation Resource Center, the overlords of architectural recovery in the Garden District about Hollie Vest:

"Her efforts have been noticed. My hat goes off to her for saving such a wonderful and historical building. It was in very bad shape. Not just anyone could have come along and given it the royal treatment like she has. We very much appreciate what she has done. And I've seen the rooms; I think it's safe to say that the guests will remember it."

A note from this author:
Katrina hit Magnolia Mansion. Hollie called me at work to make sure that she didn't miss getting in touch with me about the book. What kind of person does that when they cannot even get to their home to even see if they have a home anymore? She has become a special friend that I am glad I found.
Thank You, Hollie!

CHAPTER 3
Resurrection Mary

Chicago's most elusive ghost!

This story is courtesy of Troy Taylor—Visit his website for LOTS more "spooky" stories! http://www.prairieghosts.com
Thanks, Troy

It is a cold night in late December on the south side of Chicago. A taxicab travels along Archer Avenue as rain and sleet pelt the windshield. The driver reaches over to crank the heater up one more notch. It is the kind of night, he thinks, that makes your bones ache.

As the car rolls past the Willowbrook Ballroom, a pale figure, blurry through the wet and icy glass of the window, appears along the roadside. The driver cranes his neck and sees a young woman walking alone. She is strangely dressed for such a cold and wet night; wearing only a white cocktail dress and a thin shawl over her shoulders.

She stumbles along the uneven shoulder of the road and the cabbie pulls over and stops the car. He rolls down the window and the young girl approaches the taxi. She is beautiful, he sees, despite her disheveled appearance. Her blond hair is damp from the weather and plastered to her forehead. Her light blue eyes are the color of ice on a winter lake.

He invites her into the cab and she opens the back door and slides across the seat. The cabbie looks into the rearview mirror and asks her where she wants to go. He offers her a free ride. It's the least that he can do in this weather, he tells her.

The girl simply replies that he should keep driving down Archer Avenue, so the cabbie puts the car into gear and pulls back onto the road. He notices in his mirror that the girl is shivering so he turns up the heater again. He comments on the weather, making conversation, but she doesn't answer him at first. He wonders if she might be a little drunk because she is acting oddly.

Finally, she answers him, although her voice wavers and she sounds almost fearful. The driver is unsure if her whispered words are directed to him or if she is speaking to herself. "The snow came early this year," she murmurs and then is silent once more.

The cabbie agrees with her that it did and attempts to make more small talk with the lovely young girl. He soon realizes that she is not interested in conversation. Finally, she does speak, but when she does, she shouts at him. She orders him to pull over to the side of the road. This is where she needs to get out!

The startled driver jerks the steering wheel to the right and stops in an open area in front of two large, metal gates. He looks up and realizes where they have stopped. "You can't get out here," he says to the young woman, "this is a cemetery!"

When he looks into the rearview mirror, he realizes that he is in the cab alone...the girl is no longer in the backseat. He never heard the back door open or close, but the beautiful girl has simply disappeared.

One must wonder if it finally dawned on him just who he had taken for a ride in his cab. She is known all over the Chicago area as the region's most enigmatic and sought after ghost. Her name is "Resurrection Mary."

Chicago is a city filled with ghosts, from haunted houses to ghostly graveyards. But of all of the tales, there is one that rises above all of the others. I like to think of Resurrection Mary as Chicago's most famous ghost. It is also probably my favorite ghost story of all time. It has all of the elements of the fantastic from the beautiful female spirit to actual eyewitness sightings that have yet to be debunked. There is much about the story that appeals to me and I never tire of hearing or talking about Mary, her sightings and her mysterious origins.

Although stories of "vanishing hitchhikers" in Chicago date back to the horse and buggy days, Mary's take begins in the 1930s. It was around this time that drivers along Archer Avenue started reporting strange encounters with a young woman in a white dress. She always appeared to be real, until she would inexplicably vanish. Motorists, passing by Resurrection Cemetery, began claiming that a young woman was attempting to jump onto the running boards of their automobiles.

Over the years, there have been many sightings and encounters with the ghost alleged to be "Resurrection Mary." Dozens of young men have told of picking up the same girl, or meeting her at the ballroom, only to have her disappear from their car.

Perhaps the most believable encounter with Mary took place in 1939 and involved a young man named Jerry Palus. Below is an account of his encounter:

The Story of Jerry Palus
Aside from harried motorists who encountered Mary along Archer Avenue, one of the first people to ever meet her face to face was a young man named Jerry Palus.

His experience with Mary took place in 1939, but would leave such an impression that he would never forget it until his death in 1992. Palus remained an unshakable witness and appeared on a number of television shows to discuss his night with Resurrection Mary. Regardless, he had little to gain from his story and no reason to lie. He never doubted the fact that he spent an evening with a ghost!

Palus met the young girl at the Liberty Grove and Hall, a dance hall that was near 47th Street and Mozart. He had apparently seen her there on several occasions and finally asked her to dance one night. He did note in later interviews that he did not recall ever actually seeing the girl come into the dance hall. He looked away and then looked back a few moments later and she just seemed to appear near the wall.

Jerry asked the young woman to dance. She accepted and they spent several hours together. Strangely though, she seemed a little distant and Palus also noticed that her skin was very cold, almost icy to the touch. When he later kissed her, he found her lips were also cold and clammy.

At the end of the evening, the young woman asked Palus for a ride home and when they got to his automobile, she directed him to drive down Archer Avenue. Palus admitted to being confused. Earlier in the evening, the woman had told him where she lived and he knew that it would be far out of the way for them to travel there via Archer. When he asked her about it, she simply told him again that she wanted to go down Archer Avenue.

As they drove down the street, they approached the gates to Resurrection Cemetery and she asked him to pull over. She said that she had to get out there.

Again, Jerry was confused, not being able to understand why she would want to get out at such a spot. He agreed that he would let her out, but only if she allowed him to walk her across the street. She refused to allow this though. The beautiful girl turned in her seat and faced Palus. "This is where I have to get out," she spoke softly, "but where I'm going, you can't follow."

Palus was bewildered by this statement, but before he could respond, the girl got out of the car and ran toward the cemetery gates. She vanished before she reached them—right before Jerry's eyes! That was the moment when he knew that he had danced with a specter!

Determined to find out what was going on, Palus visited the address the girl had given him on the following day. The woman who answered the door told him that he couldn't have possibly been with her daughter the night before because she had been dead for several years. However, Palus was able to correctly identify the girl from a family portrait in the other room.

Needless to say, Palus was stunned by this revelation, but apparently, the address and identity of the woman were forgotten over the years. Some time later, when Palus was contacted again about his story (when the passage of time had renewed interest in the elusive ghost) he was unable to remember where he had gone on the day after his encounter. Despite this memory lapse, Palus' story remains the most credible of all of the Resurrection Mary encounters.

More "Resurrection Mary" Sightings

The majority of the reports seem to come from the cold winter months, like the account passed on by a cab driver.

He picked up a girl who was walking along Archer Avenue one night in 1941. It was very cold outside, but she was not wearing a coat. She jumped into the cab and told him that she needed to get home very quickly. She directed him along Archer Avenue and a few minutes later, he looked back and she was gone. He realized that he was passing in front of the cemetery when she disappeared.

In addition, to the encounters with and sightings of Mary that took place in the early years, more accounts began to surface in the middle 1900s, including many that had Mary being struck by passing cars. Drivers started reporting a young girl in white who ran out in front of their automobile. Occasionally, the girl would vanish when she collided with the car and at other times, would crumple, and fall to the road as if seriously injured. When the motorist stopped and went to help the girl, she would disappear.

In 1973, Mary was said to have shown up at least twice at a nightclub called Harlow's, on Cicero on the southwest side. She danced alone in a faded white dress and despite the fact that bouncers checked the I.D.s of everyone who came through the door, no one ever saw the girl enter or leave.

Later that same year, an annoyed cab driver entered Chet's Melody Lounge, located across Archer from the gates to

Resurrection Cemetery, looking for a fare that had skipped off without paying. The young blond woman that he reportedly picked up was nowhere to be seen. The manager explained that no blond woman had entered the bar.

During the middle 1970s, the number of Mary sightings began to increase. People from many different walks of life, from cab drivers to ministers, said they had picked her up and had given her rides. It was during this period that Resurrection Cemetery was undergoing some major renovations and perhaps this was what caused her restlessness.

On August 12, 1976, Cook County police officers investigated an emergency call about an apparent hit and run victim near the intersection of 76th Street and Roberts Road. The officers found a young female motorist in tears at the scene and they asked her where the body was that she had allegedly discovered beside the road. She pointed to a wet grassy area and the policemen could plainly see a depression in the grass that matched the shape of a human body. The girl said that just as the police car approached the scene, the body on the side of the road vanished!

In May 1978, a young couple was driving down Archer when a girl suddenly darted out in the road in front of their car. The driver swerved to avoid her but knew when he hit the brakes that it was too late. As they braced for impact, the car passed right through the girl! She then turned and ran into Resurrection Cemetery, melting right past the bars in the gate.

Another man was on his way to work in the early morning hours and spotted the body of a young girl lying directly in front of the cemetery gates. He stopped his truck and got out, quickly discovering that the woman was apparently badly injured, but still alive. He jumped into his truck and sped to the nearby police station, where he summoned an ambulance and then hurried back to the cemetery. When he came back, he found that the body was gone! However, the outline of her body was still visible on the dew-covered pavement.

On the last weekend in August 1980, Mary was seen by dozens of people, including the Deacon of the Greek Church on Archer Avenue. Many of witnesses contacted the Justice Police Department about their sightings. Squad cars were dispatched and although the police could not explain the mass sightings of a young woman who was not present when they arrived, they did find the witnesses themselves. Many of them flagged down the officers to tell them what they had just seen.

On September 5, a young man was leaving a softball game and driving down Archer Avenue. As he passed the Red Barrel Restaurant, he spotted a young woman standing on the side of the road in a white dress. He stopped the car and offered her a ride and she accepted, asking that he take her down Archer. He tried to draw her into conversation, even joking that she looked like "Resurrection Mary," but she was not interested in talking. He tried several times to get her to stop for a drink, but she never replied. He was driving past the cemetery, never having stopped or even slowed down, when he looked over and saw that the girl was gone. She had simply vanished!

In October 1989, two women were driving past Resurrection Cemetery when a girl in a white dress ran out in front of their car. The driver slammed on the brakes, sure that she was going to hit the woman, but there was no impact. Neither of the women could explain where the apparition had disappeared to.

During the 1990s, reports of Mary slacked off, but they have never really stopped altogether. Many of the roadside encounters happened near a place called Chet's Melody Lounge, which is located across the road and a little south of the cemetery gates. Because it is open into the early morning hours, it often becomes the first place where late night drivers look for the young girl who vanished before their eyes!

A number of shaken drivers have stumbled into the bar after their strange encounters, as did a cab driver in 1973. He claimed that his fare, a young woman, jumped out of the back seat of his cab without paying. She ran off and he came into Chet's because it was the closest place that she could have gone to. He told the bartender that she was an attractive blond and that she had skipped out on her fare, but imagine his surprise when staff members told him that no young woman had come in.

Another bizarre encounter took place in the summer of 1996 when the owner of the lounge, the late Chet Prusinski, was leaving the bar at around four in the morning. A man came running inside and told Chet that he needed to use the telephone. He excitedly explained that he had just run over a girl on Archer and now he couldn't find her body. Chet was skeptical about the man's story until a truck driver came in and confirmed the whole thing. He had also seen the girl but stated that she had vanished, "like a ghost." The police came to investigate but, not surprisingly, they found no trace of her.

The stories continued but perhaps the strangest account of Mary was the one that occurred on the night of August 10, 1976. This event has remained so bizarre after all this time because on this occasion, Mary did not just appear as a passing spirit. It was on this night that she left evidence behind!

A driver was passing by the cemetery around 10:30 that night when he happened to see a girl standing on the other side of the gates. He said that when he saw her, she was wearing a white dress and grasping the iron bars of the gate. The driver was considerate enough to stop down the street at the Justice Police station and alert them to the fact that someone had been accidentally locked in the cemetery at closing time. An officer responded to the call but when he arrived, there was no one there. The graveyard was dark and deserted and there was no sign of any girl.

But his inspection of the gates, where the girl had been seen standing, did reveal something. The revelation chilled him to the bone! He found that two of the bars in the gate had been pulled apart and bent at sharp angles. To make things worse, at the points on the green-colored bronze where they had been pried apart were blackened scorch marks. Within these marks was what looked to be skin texture and handprints that had been seared into the metal with incredible heat.

The marks of the small hands made big news and curiosity-seekers came from all over the area to see them. In an effort to discourage the crowds, cemetery officials attempted to remove the marks with a blowtorch, making them look even worse. Finally, they cut the bars off and installed a wire fence until the two bars could be straightened or replaced.

The cemetery emphatically denied the supernatural version of what happened to the bars. They claimed that a truck backed into the gates while doing sewer work at the cemetery and that grounds workers tried to fix the bars by heating them with a blowtorch and bending them. The imprint in the metal, they said, was from a workman trying to push them together again. While this explanation was quite convenient, it did not explain why the marks of small fingers were clearly visible in the metal.

The bars were removed to discourage onlookers, but taking them out had the opposite effect and soon, people began asking what the cemetery had to hide. The events allegedly embarrassed local officials, so they demanded that the bars be put back into place. Once they were returned to the gate, they were straightened and painted over with green paint so that the blackened area would match the other bars. Unfortunately, though, the scorched areas continued to defy all attempts to cover them and the twisted spots where the hand prints had been impressed remained obvious until just recently, when the bars were removed for good.

In July 2001, Troy Taylor, at (*http://www.prairieghosts.com*) was contacted by an unnamed witness who stated that he and his girlfriend had spotted Mary along Archer Avenue. The young woman that the witness was seeing at the time was from Lithuania and spoke only broken English. She had no information about the legend of Resurrection Mary, which makes her account of the bizarre sighting even more believable.

The couple was traveling along Archer Avenue, to take the young woman home, and spotted an odd figure near Resurrection Cemetery. The witness noted that, just before the sighting, he spotted a police officer who had pulled over a motorist on the left side of the street (down a side street). He would later use the police car as a point of reference when he and his girlfriend came back for a second look.

As they drove past, both of them spotted her walking northbound on the road with her back to their oncoming car. She was wearing a white gown that blew crisply in the wind. After the sighting had registered, the witness quickly related the legend of Mary to his girlfriend and he also called his sister on his cell phone, marking the moment of the sighting. After he explained to his date what he had seen, she insisted that they go back for another look.

The witness turned around and headed in the direction they had come from, keeping their eyes open for the woman coming toward them. In a few moments, they had passed the police car that they had seen earlier, but there was no sign of the woman in the white dress.

Suddenly, the figure seemed to lurch out from along the roadway. The witness stated that she seemed to simply appear but he couldn't be sure. She was standing along the shoulder of the road, three to five feet from the pavement, and facing their vehicle. She was dressed in a faded and discolored gown and was carrying what appeared to be a bouquet of dark flowers.

"She wasn't looking at us," the witness later recalled, "she was just staring to the south. She looked somewhat young with the blankest expression that I have ever seen on a face."

Was this Resurrection Mary or was the woman in white a part of some elaborate hoax? As far as the witness was concerned, he didn't care. "After that July, I refuse to drive by the cemetery alone," he said. "I take another route if I ever have to go that way."

During the 1990s, reports of Mary slacked off, but they have never really stopped altogether. They continue to occur today and while many of the stories are harder to believe these days, as the tales of Mary have infiltrated our culture to such a degree that almost anyone with an interest in ghosts has heard of her, some of the stories still appear to be chillingly real.

Just who is Resurrection Mary?

The most accurate version of the story of Resurrection Mary concerns a young girl who was killed while hitchhiking down Archer Avenue in the early 1930s.

Apparently, she had spent the evening dancing with a boyfriend at the O Henry Ballroom. At some point, they got into an argument and Mary (as she has come to be called) stormed out of the place. Even though it was a cold winter's night, she thought she would rather face a cold walk home than another minute with her boorish lover.

She left the ballroom and started walking up Archer Avenue. She had not gotten very far when she was struck and killed by a passing automobile. The driver fled the scene and Mary was left there to die. Her grieving parents buried her in Resurrection Cemetery, wearing a white dress and her dancing shoes. Since that time, her spirit has been seen along Archer Avenue, perhaps trying to return to her grave after one last night among the living.

It has never been known just who the earthy counterpart of Mary might have been, but several years ago a newspaper report confused things so badly that a number of writers and researchers ended up creating their own "Mary." She was another girl who was tragically killed, but had nothing to do with the woman who haunts Archer Avenue.

In the quest to learn Mary's identity, speculation fell onto a woman named Mary Bregovy, who is also buried in Resurrection Cemetery. Unfortunately, there are too many factors that prevent her from being Resurrection Mary…

Even though Bregovy was killed in an auto accident in 1934, it is unlikely that she was returning home from the O Henry Ballroom, as some have claimed. The accident in which she was killed took place on Wacker Drive in downtown Chicago. The car that she was riding in collided with an elevated train support and she was thrown through the windshield. This is very different from being killed by a hit-and-run driver on Archer Avenue.

Bregovy also did not resemble the phantom that has been reported either. According to memory and photographs, she had short, dark hair, which is the opposite of the fair-skinned blond ghost. Besides that, the undertaker, who prepared Bregovy for her funeral, recalled that she was buried in an orchid-colored dress, not the white one of legend.

However, he does add an interesting note to the story. In fact, he may have been the person who caused the confusion between spectral "Mary's" in the first place. In a newspaper interview many years ago, he mentioned that a caretaker at Resurrection Cemetery told him that he had seen a ghost on the cemetery grounds. The caretaker believed the ghost was that of Mary Bregovy.

So, who was she?

Some have speculated that she never really existed at all. They have disregarded the search for her identity, believing that she is nothing more than an "urban legend" and a piece of fascinating folklore. They believe the story can be traced to nothing more than Chicago's version of the "vanishing hitchhiker."

While the story of Resurrection Mary does bear some resemblance to the tale, the folklorists have forgotten an important thing that Mary's story has that the many versions of the other stories do not— credible eyewitness accounts, places, times and dates.

Many of these reports are not just stories that have been passed from person to person and rely on a "friend of a friend" for authenticity. In fact, some of the encounters with Mary have been chillingly up close and personal and remain unexplained to this day.

But is she really that great of a mystery? Some believe so, but many doubt that she exists at all. Who is she? No one knows but that has not stopped the stories, tales, and even songs from being spun about her. She remains an enigma and her legend lives on, not content to vanish, as Mary does when she reaches the gates to Resurrection Cemetery.

Not long after, the woman became more mysterious, and much more alluring. The strange encounters began to move further away from the graveyard and closer to the O Henry Ballroom, which is now known as the Willowbrook.

She was reported on the nearby roadway and sometimes, inside of the ballroom itself. On many occasions, young men would meet a girl at the ballroom, dance with her, and then offer her a ride home at the end of the evening. She would always accept and offer vague directions that would lead north on Archer Avenue. When the car would reach the gates of Resurrection Cemetery, the young woman would always vanish.

More common were the claims of motorists who would see the girl walking along the road. They would offer her a ride and then witness her vanishing from their car. These drivers could describe the girl in detail and nearly every single description precisely matched the previous accounts. The girl was said to have light blond hair, blue eyes and was wearing a white party dress. Some more attentive drivers would sometimes add that she wore a thin shawl, or dancing shoes, and that she had a small clutch purse.

Others had even more harrowing experiences. Rather than having the girl vanish for their car, they claimed to actually run her down in the street. They claimed to see a woman in a white dress bolt in front of their car near the cemetery and would actually describe the sickening thud as she was struck by the front of the car. When they stopped to go to her aid, she would be gone.

Some even said that the automobile passed directly through the girl. At that point, she would turn and disappear through the cemetery gates.

Bewildered and shaken drivers began to appear almost routinely in nearby businesses and even at the nearby Justice, Illinois, police station. They told strange and frightening stories; sometimes they were believed and sometimes they weren't. Regardless, they created an even greater legend of the vanishing girl, who would go on to become Resurrection Mary.

So, who is Mary and does she exist? Many remain skeptical about her, but I have found that this doesn't really seem to matter. You see, people are still seeing Mary walking along Archer Avenue at night. Drivers are still stopping to pick up a forlorn figure that seems inadequately dressed in the winter months, when encounters are most prevalent.

Curiosity-seekers still come to see the gates where the twisted and burned bars were once located and some even roam the graveyard, hoping to stumble across the place where Mary's body was laid to rest.

You see, our individual belief, or disbelief, does not really matter. Mary lives on anyway. I doubt that we will ever know who she really was, or why she haunts this peculiar stretch of roadway. And, in all honesty, I don't suppose that I ever really want to know who she was. I guess that I prefer Mary to remain just as she is…a mysterious, elusive, and romantic spirit of the Windy City.

CHAPTER 4
The Stanley Hotel

333 Wonderview Ave, P.O. Box 1767
Estes Park, CO 80517
Phone: 800-976-1377 info@stanleyhotel.com

Celebrity guests:
The Stanley Hotel, known for its architecture, magnificent setting, and famous visitors, may possibly be best known today for its inspirational role in Stephen King's novel The Shining. The hotel has been featured as one of America's most haunted hotels and with the numerous stories from visitors and staff, The Stanley Hotel continues to "shine" today, as it did in 1909 when first opened. A tour guide in 1999 reported that Stephen King witnessed a ghostly little boy wandering the halls on the second floor during his stay at the hotel in 1973. King stayed a night or two at The Stanley and began the concept of the blockbuster thriller, The Shining. King wrote the story and, against his wishes, the Jack Nicholson version was filmed at another location.

Other Celebrities Who Have Visited The Stanley

The Stanley Hotel has hosted many "famous" guests including The Unsinkable Molly Brown, John Philip Sousa, Theodore Roosevelt, the Emperor and Empress of Japan, and Robert Plant. The movie Dumb & Dumber was partially filmed at The Stanley—so Jim Carey has certainly been there during the filming of the movie.

The History of the Stanley Hotel

Forced by poor health to move West, F.O. Stanley and his famous Steamer arrived in Estes Park in 1903. Finding the town lacking in amenities, F.O. set out to change the local economy.

On the 160 acres he purchased from Lord Dunraven, Stanley first built the main building of the hotel, one of eleven buildings in the original complex. Many of those original buildings remain in use today on the remaining fifty-five acres. Where the ice pond, water reservoir, and 9-hole golf course once stood, you may now see a lone coyote or a grazing herd of elk.

Construction of the Main Building began in 1907 and took two years to complete. It was built with steel support beams and timber cut from land, now known as Rocky Mountain National Park. Most of the timber came from the Bear Lake burn in 1900, which may account for the faint smell of wood smoke that can be detected on a warm, summer day.

F.O. Stanley also helped to shape the future of tourism in Estes Park. He built the road from Lyons, over which he brought visitors, riding in a Stanley Steamer to Estes Park and The Stanley Hotel.

This marks the first time in history that an automobile, instead of a train, was used to transport people to a resort area.

By his dying year in 1940, Stanley had not only built his grand hotel, but also developed a sewer, power and water company, as well as Estes Park's first bank.

F.O. was also instrumental in helping to restore wildlife to the area, promoting the establishment of Rocky Mountain National Park and Estes Park's fairgrounds, Stanley Park.

Soon to celebrate its 100th year in operation, The Stanley Hotel continues as the most prominent fixture in Estes Park, contributing to the economic wealth and beauty of this once rustic, mountain town.

To find out more about the history, the haunting and the hotel's connection to Hollywood, join a history or ghost tour given daily.

Ghostly Sightings
The stories of ghosts are NOT on their website, but we do know that they give "Ghost Tours" at the Stanley if you are interested in a "haunted vacation." Here are a few stories that I have run across and they have been approved by The Stanley management.

The bartenders tell stories of the black-jacketed spirit of F.O. Stanley, the man who built and owned the hotel, suddenly passing by the bar or heading toward the kitchen area, then vanishing.

Registration desk staff and guests sometimes hear the piano in the music room playing by itself—probably the most told story out of the hotel, and ghostly activity at the hotel seems to increase during a full moon, according to the staff members.

A tour guide points out the two "portals" believed to be the outlets of spirits in the hotel—one being the tunnel that once led to staff quarters underground and now said to be the in-and-out door of the "otherworld." The other is the bell-tower door, with a staircase right across from the bridal suite. It's always kept closed—at least to the physical world.

Some people have seen or heard something otherworldly happen in the hotel. Lights flickering on and off, doors opening and closing by themselves, rooms getting tidied up by themselves, or strange "sit prints" on newly made beds.

The McGregor Room...
One of the cooks heard a party going on while the room was empty and two employees saw a figure appear between them as they talked. Also, something was seen and recorded moving near the door.

Room 217
Stephen King and his wife found their clothes and luggage had been rearranged, after a short absence.

Room 203
A big loot of items that were reported lost turned up in room 203.
Room 1302
Tables and chairs have been seen moving on their own.
Room 1312
A housekeeper discovered lamps and pictures on the floor of a room that had just been cleaned. A man's voice was heard in room 1312.
The Fourth Floor...
On the fourth floor, children have been seen playing in the corridor. In the lobby, books have been seen flying off the shelves. A homeless woman haunts the concert hall, where unexplained shrieking has been heard.
The Third Floor...
One visitor checked into The Stanley and was taken to her room on the third floor. Immediately after she walked into the room, the lights were flickering. Not thinking anything of it, she placed her belongings in the room and turned her back for a few moments while she was getting ready to settle in for the night.

As she turned back around, everything had been moved! She called down to the front desk to ask if anyone else was in the room. Her answer was, 'No.' Well, she went on to bed and was awakened about midnight by the noise of kids running up and down the hall. She opened the door, but nobody was there...however, the noise moved into her room. She said the sounds of lots of children at play filled her room.

Frozen in fear, the woman watched as her belongings appeared as though someone were moving them. This continued until daybreak.
Room 412
Shadows have been seen and the bed has been known to shake.

Tour guides have confirmed that at least one child on the third floor is seen frequently. It is there where the guests have claimed they saw a little girl running up and down the halls all night, or crying in the corner.

Room 401

A tour guide dramatizes the story of the newlyweds that stayed in the bridal suite…Room 401, seven years ago.

The bride awoke and found a man standing in the corner of the room watching the couple. The apparition walked slowly toward the bed, approaching her new husband's side. It picked up her husband's wedding ring from the nightstand and, with an evil grin, tossed it down the bathroom sink, and disappeared. Frantic, the woman called the manager. Hotel staff was able to salvage the ring. The manager offered to buy the couple a drink at what was then the Dunraven Grille, named for a scandalous fellow known to Estes Park in the early 20th century.

On leaving the bar, the new bride fell to her knees crying as soon as she set her eyes on the large portrait of the late Lord Dunraven hanging in the lobby. That, she said, was the man who had visited Room 401.

And Let's Not Forget F. O. and Flora…

In addition to its regular guests, the hotel is said to play host to a number of other worldly visitors. The most notable is F.O. Stanley himself who is most often seen in the lobby and the Billiard Room, which was his favorite room when he was still alive.

On one such occasion, he was said to have appeared during a tour group's visit to the Billiard Room, materializing behind a member of the tour.

Bartenders at the old hotel also report having seen F.O. stroll through the bar, disappearing when they try to cut him off at the kitchen.

Not to be left out, Flora Stanley haunts the hotel as well, continuing to entertain guests with her piano playing in the ballroom.

While there are no documented murders or deaths at the hotel, the stories that come out of there sound as though there are almost as many ghosts as there are guests, huge wedding parties, and staff

combined. *The stories are retold in local ghost books by former guests and former and current staff. The ghost stories are numerous; however, they've taken on a life of their own.*

Come and visit our lovely hotel!

REDRUM
MURDER

CHAPTER 5
Willard Library

21 First Avenue Evansville, IN 47710
Phone: 812-425-4309 Fax: 812-421-9742
Email: willard@willard.lib.in.us

Is Willard Library Haunted?

Countless employees and patrons have reported seeing an apparition, each giving an eerily similar description. Is the legend true? We will leave that for you to decide.

Who Is the Ghost?

Numerous speculations and opinions exist about whose ghost the famed "lady in grey" actually is. Some believed that the ghost emigrated from a nearby cemetery. Others say that a woman died in the building during its early days and that she liked the library so much that she never left (and gets jealous when mortals read her treasured books).

Some say it's Louise Carpenter, daughter of the library's founder, Willard Carpenter. While Willard provided for his family upon his death, Louise was very unhappy when he left most of his estate to the new library. She sued the library's Board of Trustees, claiming that her father was "of unsound mind and was unduly influenced in establishing Willard Library." She lost the suit, and as a result, her claim to any of the library's property.

Some people say that after her death, her spirit returned to the place that caused her so much grief during her life…Willard Library, where she roams in silence.

Those who believe this opinion say that she will continue to haunt the library until the property and its holdings are turned back over to the living heirs of the Willard Carpenter family.

Others disagree. The Grey Lady is not malevolent, as they assume Louise would be. In fact, library employees have come to see the Lady in Grey as another staff member. They know that every so often, they will see the Grey Lady.

And they do see her…often. There are reports of hundreds, perhaps thousands, of ghostly encounters. Sometimes her presence is accompanied by the strong scent of musky perfume. Other times, she makes her presence known by moving books, adjusting lights, and turning faucets on and off. She is not malevolent, but she has many ways to let the world know she is here.

One day, we may find out who is haunting the Willard Library. Until then, **watch quietly.** Perhaps you'll see our Lady in Grey as she passes in front of our cameras…

Some Other Notable Sightings and Strange Happenings

The famed "lady in grey" did return, however. She has appeared many times to many different people in many different ways since that cold winter night in 1937:

Numerous current and former Willard staff members have reported seeing a shadowy grey female apparition that appears suddenly and then vanishes into thin air.

A former librarian, alone in the library after closing time, suddenly heard water running forcefully on the second floor. She discovered that the faucet in the bathroom had been mysteriously turned on.

In the spring of 1983, the faucet in the second floor lavatory turned itself on while one of the librarians was actually in the room.

Two members of the Tri-State Genealogy Society, working alone in the library on, ironically enough, cemetery records were overcome with an unexplained strong scent of heavy perfume. (Note: Parapsychologists, scientists that study hauntings and apparitions, say that strange scents accompanying spectral manifestations are not at all uncommon).

Ghosts on TV

The Willard Library has also been featured on television. In addition to our local broadcasts, the Lady in Grey has been featured on cable TV nationwide. Some of these shows include:

Sci-Fi Channel
Proof Positive (Episode 106)
Discovery Channel; Real Ghost Hunters
PBS; Across Indiana
Family Channel

The Ghost Stories
Winter 1937: The first sighting of Willard Library's "Lady in Grey"

On a cold, snow-covered night in the winter of 1937, the library's janitor, as was his nightly routine, came to the building at 3:00 a.m. to shovel coal into the heating furnace, ensuring warmth for the coming busy day.

Armed with his flashlight and gun, the janitor cautiously made his way to the unlit basement to fuel the fire. Though comfortable in his duty, he was always wary of any unexpected nighttime visitors.

Suddenly, as he neared the furnace, he froze motionless and dropped his flashlight to the dusty basement floor. A look of amazement and fear overcame the normally docile janitor's face.

Standing before him in that dark and dreary basement of Willard Library was a ghostly veiled lady dressed in glowing grey. In his astonishment, he managed to bend down and pick up his flashlight, noticing that even her shoes were grey.

Before the janitor could regain his composure, the image disappeared and he was once again in silent solitude.

Frightened and confused, the janitor completely forgot about shoveling that coal into the furnace. He ran crazily from the basement.

Although he saw her many times after that first sighting, he never felt good about seeing this specter. In fact, he is the only person to ever leave the library's employment and specifically give the ghost sightings as his reason for quitting.

Of course, nobody believed him. He took to drink because of seeing her, and the townspeople thought he was crazy, or just a drunk. It's a shame, because this custodian was the first person to report seeing the ghost, and he was the first to say that the ghost was a woman.

Staff Encounters
There have been a large number of unexplained incidents witnessed by Willard's staff members. Several are recounted here…

Carol Bartlett and David, her co-worker, were straightening up at closing time on a Sunday afternoon. David was arranging the chairs around the tables. Carol had been working in another area, and when she came to where David had been straightening up, she found one of the chairs pushed away from the table. She pushed it back where it belonged. Not more than five minutes later, they found the chair pushed out again.

While Carol had been somewhat dubious about her co-worker's claimed ghost encounters, she had now experienced something very unusual herself.

Lyn Martin, who is now head of special collections for the library, saw a file box move off its shelf and fall in a lovely arch. She had been behind the counter. Another staff member was standing in front of it. It looked almost as if the file had jumped, rather than having been pushed. The file spilled its contents onto the floor in the perfect shape of a fan. Lyn was surprised, to say the least, by this rather unusual occurrence.

Anne Wills, the Children's Librarian, was alone in the children's room. She was wearing long, dangling earrings. She felt someone behind her pull her hair back and touch the earring on one ear. When she turned to see who it was, nobody was there.

Anita Glover has had a couple of experiences with the Lady in Grey. At the time, she was the assistant children's librarian and Joan Elliot Parker was the special collections librarian. Joan had gone into the old women's bathroom in the basement and locked the door behind her. The faucet turned on; Joan turned it off. At the same time, Anita noticed her security camera showing someone there, but not quite visible, moving quickly down the hallway.

Greg Hager, Director for the Willard Library, once smelled very strong perfume in the men's room. He checked to see if any of the women had recently gone in to restock supplies, but nobody had. Many others have reported similar olfactory incidents, and those experienced in these things claim that the strong smell of perfume often accompanies the presence of a ghost.

Greg also reports there have been strange electrical encounters. For example, light bulbs will go off and on by themselves even though the lights are on the same electrical circuit. One evening, the whole building was doing that, with no obvious explanation. He says that a lot of people have reported having problems with recording and video equipment.

Margaret Maier was the children's librarian at the Willard for nearly 50 years. She first saw the Grey Lady in the late 1950s, and told of many encounters during her years working there. Margaret came to see the ghost as a companion, perhaps even a friend.

Margaret told Betty Palmer, another long-time Willard staff member, about an incident that occurred in 1985. Margaret and her sister Ruth were previewing the Easter Egg Tree for a group of women and their children. A little boy wandered towards the stairs, away from the group. His mother tried to get him to return, but he said he was afraid of the ghost.

The little boy was only three years old. We don't know if he had heard about the ghost before his visit to Willard, but he was certainly aware of her presence by the time he left.

Betty also recounts another incident that Margaret had told her. During the 1980 remodeling of the library's children's room, Margaret believed the Grey Lady followed her to the home she shared with her sister Ruth.

One night, Ruth woke Margaret in the middle of the night, and as soon as she awoke, she could smell the musky aroma of the Grey Lady's perfume. On a different evening, Margaret told of clearly seeing the ghost in her living room wearing a gray pleated, woolen skirt. Ruth also caught a ghostly glimpse that same evening. A few days later, Margaret's nephew saw the ghost, but mistook it for his aunt. When he called to ask her why she was dressed wearing gray clothes and old-style button-top boots, his aunt came into the room and he could simultaneously see both the ghost and his aunt. Although her nephew had doubted the existence of the Grey Lady, he was convinced now that she was quite real.

Margaret is the one who insists that Willard's ghost be known as the Grey Lady, and that grey should be spelled in the British manner with an 'e' rather than with an 'a' as is generally preferred in America.

Greg Hager, the director for Willard Library, recalls one incident where he was meeting with a television reporter to talk about an upcoming book sale. During the interview, a couple of staff members who had been working in the children's room, came up to them. One was very upset and visibly shaking.

The assistant librarian had been selecting children's materials for the book sale and had taken the selected materials to log them into the computer. It took only a few moments to complete the computer work.

When they returned to the shelves, they discovered that every fourth book or so had been partially pulled out and was jutting out from its shelf at an angle. Several hundred books, across several bookshelves, had been rearranged in this fashion.

Greg estimates it would have taken an experienced librarian ten to fifteen minutes to do something like this, but the library workers had been away from the stacks for only a few moments. There were no other people in the children's area at that time.

The television reporter interviewed one of the women, but the other wasn't interested in being interviewed. The camera operator taped the interview, and took video footage of the rearranged books. The reporter called Greg after returning to the studio. Now she was upset. She told him the video of Greg's interview about the book sale was intact, but the footage of the interview with the woman who had been working in the children's room was completely blank, as was the video showing the rearranged bookshelves.

To compound this unfortunate circumstance, all of this activity took place just outside of the view of the existing ghost cam. None of this unusual activity was recorded.

Paranormal Investigators

Willard Library has been host to a number of paranormal investigators. Sometimes these investigations appear to be very rigorous scientific experiments.

For example, one grouped checked for electro-magnetic field (EMF) fluctuations, some have shot infrared images. One came in with a specialized infrared device and actually found "orbs" flitting about like butterflies. They claim to have found up to eight or nine different entities existing in the library.

Paranormal investigations are now scheduled once a year. There have been ten or twelve such investigations so far, and the once-per-year slots are booked until 2009 with groups wanting to research the Willard's ghost.

Meet the Willard Staff:
Greg Hager, Director
Kathy Simpson, Business Manager
Eva V. Sanford, Adult Services Librarian
Tina Sizemore, Children's Librarian
Lyn Martin, Special Collections Librarian
John C. Scheer, Technical Services Librarian
Pat Sides, Archivist

CHAPTER 6
Hotel Del Coronado

1500 Orange Avenue
Coronado, California 92118
Phone: 619-552-8041 Fax: 619-522-8491
idonoho@hotelDel.com

The Ghost Story

Kate Morgan, a pretty woman in her mid 20s, checked into the Hotel Del Coronado alone on Thursday, November 24, 1892 (Thanksgiving evening.) During her stay, hotel employees—many of whom had frequent interactions with Kate—reported that she had appeared ill and very unhappy. She had told quite a few employees that she was waiting for her brother, who she said was a doctor, to join her...but he never showed up.

Five days after she checked in, Kate was found dead on an exterior staircase leading to the beach. Kate had a gunshot wound to her head, which the coroner later determined was self-inflicted.

A search of her hotel room revealed no personal belongings. In fact, there was nothing to identify the "beautiful stranger" except the name she used when she registered: Lottie A. Bernard (from Detroit).

After her death, police sent a sketch of Kate's face and information about her death to newspapers and police stations around the country in hopes that someone could shed light on "the dark mystery surrounding the suicide of the unknown girl at the Coronado Hotel."

Eventually, Lottie Bernard was identified as Kate Morgan, originally from Iowa and wife of Tom Morgan. Reportedly, Tom Morgan was a gambler, who may have made his living gambling on the railroad.

After the inquest into Kate's suicide, a gentleman came forward to say that he had seen Kate arguing with a man (thought to have been Tom) on a train en route to San Diego. The witness said that Tom disembarked before reaching San Diego. Kate continued on to the Hotel Del Coronado by herself where, it is assumed, she waited for Tom to join her. When he never showed up, Kate took her own life.

Since Kate's death, stories of ghostly happenings have been circulating at The Del. Hotel guests, employees, and even paranormal researchers have attested to some supernatural occurrences at the hotel.

Witnesses report flickering lights, televisions that turn on and off by themselves, dramatic shifts in room temperatures, odd scents, unexplained voices, the sound of strange footsteps, mysterious breezes, (which cause curtains to billow when windows are closed) and objects that move of their own accord; still others claim to have seen the ghost of Kate Morgan herself.

Ghostly Encounters
As told by Christine Donovan, at The Del, and author of Beautiful Stranger: The Ghost of Kate Morgan and the Hotel Del Coronado

Through the years, hotel guests and employees have reported a variety of ghostly activities in Room 3327 (this is the room Kate Morgan stayed in, although it was numbered 302 at that time).

Activity has also been reported in room 3519, although there is no known connection between room 3519 and Kate Morgan. However, there was a story circulating that a hotel maid actually witnessed Kate's death and then mysteriously disappeared...never to be seen or heard from again.

While it is amazing that the hotel housekeeper, who attended Kate, was not interviewed during the inquest (nor did the newspapers ever seem to get in touch with her), so there is nothing to support this story.

Like many other myths, this version of Kate's death is multilayered. Because this maid supposedly witnessed Kate's death, the spirit of the unidentified housekeeper is said to haunt The Del in Room 3519 (which, as the story goes, was the maid's room).

Here are a few episodes that have been documented in the recent past:

Mr. & Mrs. R., Lake Elsinore, CA...Room 3327...February, 2002:

Mrs. R. and her husband decided to spend a long Valentine's weekend at The Del. Unfortunately; the Victorian Building (where they had wanted to stay) was completely sold out, except for the first night of their planned weekend getaway. As a result, they made reservations for one night in the Victorian Building and the remaining nights in the hotel's Ocean Towers.

The day Mr. and Mrs. R. checked in had been rainy and cold, which made their room even more inviting, so they decided to stay in and order room service.

Later that evening, a hotel manager came by to ask them if anything had been unintentionally left in their bathroom (possibly by a hotel employee.) The male manager was accompanied by a female housekeeper. While the manager went to check out the bathroom, the housekeeper kept her distance, peering into the room from the hallway.

After dinner, Mrs. R. took a shower when she noticed that the bathroom lights were dimming and flickering off and on. After her shower, Mr. R. took a shower. While he was showering, Mrs. R. noticed that the tassel on the room's ceiling fan began circulating "as if someone had walked by and brushed it."

Later on, while both Mr. and Mrs. R. were in bed asleep, their bedcovers were jerked off the bed. Mrs. R., who thought her husband was just hogging the blankets, went right back to sleep.

In the morning, Mr. R. asked his wife, "Did you see what happened here last night?" Mrs. R. had no idea what her husband was talking about. He then told her that someone standing at the foot of the bed, where he could see the outline of a female head and body, had pulled off their covers. To make matters worse, as he was lying in bed, too afraid to go back to sleep, Mr. R. began hearing the guestroom doorknob rattling. Though he felt drawn to find out what was causing the noise, Mr. R. couldn't bring himself to go to the door.

Only after Mr. R. told his story, did Mrs. R. tell her husband about having seen the room's fan tassel moving inexplicably the night before.

Imagine Mrs. R.'s surprise when her husband told her that he had witnessed a similar thing after she had fallen to sleep. He told her that the fan tassel began to move as if someone had walked by and batted it.

Perplexed by these events, Mr. and Mrs. R. said a little prayer for what they imagined was the "troubled spirit" in Room 3327. Afterward they called a hotel bellman to help move them into their Ocean Towers room for the remainder of their stay.

When the bellman arrived, he greeted them by saying, "Well, what was it like to sleep in the haunted room?" And that was the first either one of them had ever heard anything about a Hotel Del Coronado ghost! Mrs. R. later reasoned that the hauntedness might have explained the housekeeper's unwillingness to come into the room the night before, preferring to wait in the hallway instead.

Curiously, Mrs. R. later reported that she had one of the most peaceful night's sleep in her entire life in Room 3327. She remembers having "wonderful dreams" with "children's laughter." However, although Mr. and Mrs. R. were more saddened than unnerved by their experiences in room 3327, they admitted that they do not intend to ever stay in that room again.

A postscript: Three weeks after their Del visit, as Mr. and Mrs. R. were recalling the strange goings-on they had experienced at The Del, the phone rang. It was a call informing Mr. and Mr. R. that they had been chosen as the grand-prize winners in a contest.

The prize? A trip for two to the Hotel Del Coronado! They were thrilled, but when they made their reservations, they made it very clear that they were willing to stay in "any room except 3327."

WW, San Diego, CA...Room 3327...January 2000:

A doorman, WW, along with a female concierge, had the opportunity to show off the haunted room to two young guests. After they arrived in the room, WW noticed that the bedcovers needed straightening. It was obvious that a woman had been lying on one side of the bed and had not straightened the covers after she had gotten up.

This, in itself, struck WW as very odd, since the room had been thoroughly cleaned and was in every way ready for its next guests.

WW walked over to the bed to straighten out the covers, but when he tried to fix them, he could not undo the impression of the woman's body. The guests, as well as the concierge, began screaming, and everyone immediately left the room! WW was totally baffled.

About the two young visitors, WW said that they were a little scared, but they were also very mystified and intrigued about what they had witnessed.

CCM, Mooresville, NC...September 1993...

CCM, who is an anesthetist by profession, was living in Minnesota in September 1993, when she made her first trip to The Del. She stayed in a suite in the Victorian Building at the western corner, facing the ocean, on the second or third floor.

After a lovely dinner in the Crown Room, CCM retired for the night. In the middle of the night, as she often did, CCM got up from bed to get a drink of water.

As she was idly looking out the window, CCM noticed a woman

walking down some exterior stairs toward the ocean. CCM assumed the woman was in "period costume" since she was wearing a white blouse with a long dark skirt. Her hair was long and dark.

All of a sudden, the woman turned around and looked directly at CCM. CCM was taken aback, wondering how it was possible that the lady on the beach could look directly into the hotel room. CCM's room was in total darkness; there were no lights on, and there was no way for the woman on the beach to be able to see CCM, yet CCM knew that the woman was looking right at her. The experience was so "unnerving" that CCM mentioned it to her future husband the next day.

That same day, as her future husband was checking out, CCM went into the hotel gift shop to purchase some postcards. There she saw a book about the hotel, with a picture of a woman who looked just like the woman CCM had seen the night before. CCM purchased the book, but really didn't think any more about it until she started to thumb through the book about two days later.

The book CCM purchased, which tells the story of Kate Morgan, contained specific information about where Kate's body was found. Only then did CCM realize that the woman she had seen, looking just like Kate Morgan, was also "walking in Kate's footsteps." That's when CCM realized that she might have seen a ghost!

In retrospect, CCM believes that her middle-of-the-night state of mind, when you wake up and you don't have your defense mechanisms up, made her more receptive to a ghostly encounter. Although CCM did not know ahead of time that The Del had a resident ghost, CCM does believe in the possible existence of paranormal phenomena.

KL, Irvine, CA...June 1982...

KL was part of a four-couple group that was celebrating the 35th birthday of one of their friends. After dinner in town, the eight friends walked back to the hotel.

When KL got to her guestroom at The Del, she glanced at the door next to hers and saw a beautiful woman there. KL says, "I glanced. She glanced. I smiled. She smiled. I went into my room. She went into her room."

Immediately upon entering her room, however, KL suddenly realized that she had seen something special. Unfortunately, when KL looked in the hallway again, the vision had vanished.

"The woman was beautiful with her dark hair pulled up in the back. She was wearing a beautiful dress—fitted waist, high collar, tucks down the front, with sheer sleeves, in voile like fabric. But there was no color to her or her clothes. It was all sort of whitish-gray and almost transparent. It was as if there was no life."

KL wasn't sad or scared about the apparition. Instead, she remembers a wonderful "peaceful feeling." Only afterward did KL realize that she had just seen a ghost.

KL had been studying metaphysics at the time, and she feels that she was particularly open to the spiritual world at that point in her life. Five years later, KL did come across a book that featured The Del's ghost, but up until then, she was unaware that The Del had a ghost. She says, "People may imagine that ghosts are always sad, but the Kate I saw was happy."

Computer Executive from the East Coast...Room 3327...1999, 2000, 2001...

When a computer executive from the East Coast made his first reservation at The Del in 1999, he asked to stay in the haunted room. Although this guest never saw Kate during his visit, he did experience endlessly quirky events, most of them having to do with failed electrical systems.

First off, each time this gentleman tried to confirm his reservation, he was told that there was no reservation for him in the computer (fortunately, the hotel was always able to retrieve the reservation "manually"). For instance, when he called a week before his stay: "no reservation." When he called from an airport en route to San Diego, the same response. And even after he arrived at The Del and tried to check in: "no reservation."

His Del room keys, which are electronic, failed again and again and again, had to be reprogrammed, and reissued a number of times. The lights in his room also dimmed and grew brighter repeatedly, with no apparent explanation.

Upon hearing these stories, a coworker suggested that the gentleman "challenge" the ghost by telling it something like, "If you're really a ghost, let me see you throw a towel into the bathtub!" Though the gentleman in 3327 ignored this suggestion, later that day, a towel mysteriously appeared in the middle of his bathtub; the next day, the same thing happened.

At the end of his 1999 stay, the gentleman was unable to access the hotel's televised checkout system and had to go to the front desk to conduct his final bit of business.

During his 2000 visit in the ghost room, this same gentleman experienced exasperating phone problems. Every day—sometimes more than once a day—his phone would ring, he would answer it, and there would be absolutely nothing there, no sound of someone hanging up, no dial tone, etc. His phone message light would also come on even when there was no message. During the last night of his stay, his phone rang at 4:00 a.m.; he answered it and there was no one there so he shouted at Kate to cease and desist! With that, the electric alarm clock rang exactly three times. Not only hadn't the alarm clock been set to go off, if it had been set to go off, it would have done so at 6:30 a.m., not 4:00 a.m.

Finally, during his most recent stay in 2001, he recalls this eerie experience: When I checked into the room, there was the very clear imprint of someone lying on the bed. The phone also continued to give him problems in 2001: it rang and no one was there, or the message light wouldn't come on when he actually had a message. In addition, problems with electric lights continued to plague him—they turned off and on by themselves; or, after leaving his room with the lights left on, he would return to find them turned off.

As a side-note, he and his wife stayed in room 3519 during a 1999 visit. One morning they awoke to find freshly cut roses outside their door with no note or explanation.

According to a 1992 interview with former hotel public relations director, a Secret Service agent was assigned to Room 3519 in 1983, during George Bush's vice presidency, he called the front desk to complain about the noise from the room above (loud footsteps and talking). When the attendant at the front desk told the agent that there was no room above his room (he was on the top floor), the Secret Service agent asked to change rooms.

Christine points out that Kate's room sees a lot of paranormal activity, which has been reported by guests as well as employees. Some of our "ghost sighters" have also encountered Kate in other hotel locations, including along hallways or on the beach.

Although Kate seems to be more of a prankster than an evil spirit, this generally affable apparition has been known to display a decidedly spooky side.

Christine said that one of the guests spent a restless night in Kate's room, during which doorknobs rattled, lights flickered off and on, and a ghostly image ripped the bedcovers right off the bed!

Not thinking much about it, the employee walked over to the bed, grabbed the bedspread, and started to pull. Much to everyone's amazement, the imprint remained, as if someone were still lying on top of the bed. Christine says that it scared the employees and the guests, who took off running and never looked back!

According to Christine, news of ghost sightings usually reaches her in roundabout ways. A guest will happen to mention something to an employee, or a visitor will write something on a guest comment card. Eventually, the report reaches her.

For instance, a man from Irvine, California wrote on a guest comment card that he had been staying in Kate Morgan's room with his wife when he was "awakened by the rustling of petticoats and skirts...and the shuffling of feet along carpet."

Another guest sent the hotel an e-mail after his ghostly encounter at The Del. As Christine describes, this was an energy-conscious family, who turned off everything before leaving the room, but when they returned, everything was on, including the television. These same guests reported a steady stream of what they characterized as "fluke happenings" throughout their stay. The guests, who came from Oregon, weren't staying in the ghost room, but as Christine points out, the hotel's supernatural sightings aren't confined to Kate's room alone.

In fact, not all of The Del's paranormal activity can even be attributed to Kate. A hotel housekeeper reported that she saw a male figure appear and then disappear in Palm Court; an area located right off the lobby. The man, who was dressed in contemporary clothes (often times sightings include figures in period dress), returned again three weeks later and then two weeks after that, always dressed the same, appearing suddenly and then disappearing.

Another guest caught sight of a ghostly male figure in the Babcock & Story Bar. She saw a very, very tall man, pencil thin, with a long neck, small face and beard, dressed in clothes from the 1800s.

How does Christine separate those stories that seem more fiction than fact? She says that she has only talked to one or two people whose stories she did not believe. Otherwise, the ghost-sighters tend to be solid citizens who relate interesting, but not outlandish, tales of paranormal activity.

In fact, Christine claims that it is the decidedly undramatic aspects of most of the stories that has made a believer out of her. For instance, a doctor e-mailed her that during his stay, his shoes and socks, which he always carefully placed by his bedside at night, would end up all over the room by the time he woke up. In my mind, that's not enough of a story to have made up. In addition, it fits very well with other paranormal accounts she has heard about objects being tossed about a room, seemingly for no reason at all.

A British film crew was covering The Del's ghost story for "Dead Famous," a long-running television series in England. Apparently, while the crew was filming in Kate's room, a skeptic became sickly, eventually becoming too shaken to stand up or even remain in the room. Later she admitted that this had been her first paranormal experience ever, saying that she had been overcome by a frightening sense of Kate's final moments!

Another guest reported that Kate's initials seemed to be drawn in the steamy bathroom mirror. Still another guest was kept awake by spooky "whisper-yelling" from a source he could not identify.

The Del's vintage shop experiences more than its share of paranormal activity, mostly in the form of merchandise "flying" off the walls and shelves.

According to Christine, the hotel's retail department no longer tries to use one section of the store because display items never stay put. Two shoppers contacted Christine with their supernatural experience, reporting that their camera failed to work inside the store, where they experienced chilly air (a common paranormal phenomenon), followed by alternating waves of fear and relief.

In fact, several other guests believed that they have been "overtaken" by Kate's spirit. One guest felt that he was "grabbed hold of," once in the middle of the night and, during another visit, in the evening on the beach. In each case, the gentleman experienced bouts of shaking and sweating.

Ghostly photography has also been finding its way to The Del. A Phoenix resident was surprised to see that the outline of a Victorian woman seemed to be superimposed on a photo she had taken during her visit.

A number of guests report that inexplicable orbs of light show up on their Del photography. Christine says that she has seen quite a few of these, and is inclined to think that these are the result of operator error or errors in development or are even due to quirks in the cameras themselves. Still, she does hear repeatedly from the photographers themselves that this is a Del-only phenomenon, something that has never occurred before or since—even on the same roll of film.

Christine believes that she has experienced the exasperating effects of Kate's spirit during a variety of on-site television interviews. Christine says that, inevitably, the camera, sound or light equipment will fail. It's happened so many times that she now advises incoming production crews to bring plenty of back-up equipment and replacement parts because things that "never go wrong" anywhere else, routinely go wrong when filming stories about The Del's ghost.

Not surprisingly, the media has closely followed the legend of Kate Morgan, and the stories about The Del's ghost have appeared nationally and internationally in newspapers, magazines, and on television.

Christine does not expect The Del's ghost to end anytime soon. Even though she believes, there are only a relative handful of people who can experience the supernatural, The Del plays host to thousands and thousands of visitors a year, so it's always inevitable that one of the guests will eventually cross paths with one of the resident spirits.

Never having encountered Kate personally, Christine says that suits her just fine. She says that she always says there are two kinds of people in the world—those that would like to see a ghost and those that would not. She definitely is in the second group.

You can pick up a copy of Christine's book, *"Beautiful Stranger: The Ghost of Kate Morgan and the Hotel Del Coronado"* online at www.Delshop.com. The Del sent me a copy and it was FANTASTIC!

HISTORY OF THE HOTEL DEL CORONADO

The Del, which was designed as it was being built, first opened its doors in 1888, after only eleven months of construction.

The United States of America looked far different than it does today. At that time, California was separated from the rest of the country by vast unsettled territories.

The 1848 discovery of gold in northern California had propelled settlement to the West Coast, but even forty years later, much of America's interior was still unsettled. Imagine what it must have been like for the hotel's early guests to leave the comforts and culture of the east and travel through the vast remoteness of the west to reach The Del.

In the early days, most guests traveled to The Del by train, and a trip from the east took seven days. Wealthy travelers journeyed in relative luxury, the wealthiest of who had their own private rail cars that were hitched up to trains back east and unhitched when they reached The Del. To accommodate private rail cars, the hotel had a spur track on property.

Not only was the hotel part of the movement west, it was part of a way of life, which was epitomized by America's luxurious railroad resorts. These were the watering holes for the rich, the famous, and the privileged. In fact, the hotel's early patrons very likely spent their days traveling by train from one fabulous resort to another. At one time, the Hotel Del Coronado was one of many such resorts; today, it is one of the few that has not only survived, but still flourishes as a wonderful world-class hotel.

The Del was conceived and built by two mid-western businessmen, who became acquainted after moving to San Diego in the mid 1880s. In 1885, Elisha Babcock and Hampton Story bought the entire undeveloped peninsula of Coronado. They then subdivided the land, sold off the lots, recouped their money, and proceeded to build what they envisioned would be the "talk of the Western world."

Promoted as a fishing and hunting resort, the waters that surrounded The Del were rich with marine life; the nearby scrub was filled with quail, rabbit, and other small game (and the hotel's chef was happy to cook a guest's catch of the day). But, in addition to these pursuits, the hotel offered more refined amenities including billiards (separate facilities for men and women), bowling, croquet, swimming, boating, bicycling, archery, golf, and fine dining. There were also special rooms set aside for smoking, reading, writing, cards, chess, and music.

The Del also showcased a lot of modern technology: it was lighted by electricity (at that time, it was one of the largest buildings in the country to have electric lights); there were telephones (but not in the guests' rooms), and there were elevators. There was a fire alarm system and state-of-the-art fire fighting equipment (although it is not known to have ever been used). There were also numerous bathrooms, all equipped with something very rare: water pressure. The hotel was outfitted in fine china and linen from Europe. Furnishings came from the east, as did many of the original employees.

The Hotel Del Coronado became a mecca for sophisticated eastern travelers, who had grown a little bored with the resorts on that side of the country, and who looked for exciting alternatives to European travel.

In 1906, polo was added, and in 1913, the hotel opened its own school for the children of long-term guests, many of whom would stay at The Del for months at a time. The early 1900s also brought the addition of "Tent City," which was developed by The Del for America's new emerging social segment: the middle class. Tent City, which lasted until 1939, was located on hotel property just south of The Del and offered modest tent and bungalow accommodations at reasonable rates.

The hotel's heyday continued into the 1920s, although by then, the clientele had shifted. There had been a war, and federal income tax had been instituted. No longer were there so many people who could pack up their families, their belongings, and their servants, and while away a season at The Del.

Times had changed. Now, women bobbed their hair, rolled up their skirts, rolled down their hose, took up smoking, and took off in rumble seats—and the men took off after them. The Roaring Twenties was truly the party decade at The Del, with lots of Hollywood coming to call, including people like Charlie Chaplin. But, he wasn't the only luminary. Even England's Prince of Wales visited The Del during the twenties, as did Lindbergh, who was honored at the hotel after his historic 1927 solo transatlantic flight.

During the Depression, the hotel suffered some, but not as much as many other turn-of-the-century resorts, which could not survive such hard times. Fortunately, the strong military economy in San Diego helped keep The Del afloat. In fact, the hotel continued to draw guests all through the Thirties, despite the Depression.

When World War II began, Coronado—like so many other areas on the West Coast—panicked, and so did the hotel's guests. Visitors wanted to get off Coronado and out of California as quickly as possible, but Coronado was still serviced by ferries only, so getting out fast was practically impossible.

During the war, blackout laws went into effect as Coronado's military base swelled with new recruits. Part of The Del was used by the Navy for housing and the hotel became a magnet for military men and their sweethearts. Couples danced at The Del, romanced at The Del, partied at The Del, married at The Del, honeymooned at The Del, and eventually returned after the war to celebrate at The Del.

Meanwhile, all across America, more and more nineteenth century resorts were being abandoned or destroyed. Like The Del, most were used by the military during the war, and some were even taken over entirely—for hospitals, for housing, for internment centers, even for reasons never disclosed. Afterwards, many of these hotels could not rebound.

The post-war years were no more generous. After World War II, Americans turned away from the past and tradition. They were interested in the future and whatever was new…televisions, TV dinners, suburbia, shiny new automobiles…and, with the automobiles came fast food restaurants, drive-in movies, and motels.

Still, The Del prevailed, thanks to a series of owners during the fifties and sixties who wanted to keep her going. During some of those leaner years, the hotel took in "resident guests." These guests were people who lived at The Del from one year to the next and their rent usually included all meals.

Although the "Grand Lady by the Sea" may have been a little bit worse for wear at this time, she was still able to cast her magic spell far and wide. In 1958, director Billy Wilder chose The Del for the filming of Some Like It Hot, starring another timeless American legend, Marilyn Monroe.

Fortunately, by the late Sixties and into the Seventies, Americans had a change of heart, as they became more interested in history and more interested in saving their history. During this period, The Del was brought back to her former glory and has enjoyed good years ever since. In fact, since that time, every president since Lyndon Johnson has visited the hotel.

The Del is proud to have a permanent place in the nation's history and honored to serve a new generation of travelers.

FAMOUS VISITORS AT THE HOTEL DEL CORONADO

Since it opened in 1888, the Hotel Del Coronado has played host to a passing parade of famous patrons from every walk of life. There have been presidents, princes, glitterati, and literati.

Presidents

Benjamin Harrison (1889-1893): Ten presidents have visited the Hotel Del Coronado, starting with President Benjamin Harrison, who was touring the country by train and had breakfast at The Del on April 23, 1891 (supposedly he greeted San Diego well-wishers in his dressing robe and slippers from the back of his rail car). This was the first time an in-office president had visited San Diego. A Delegation of California politicians, hosted by Governor Henry H. Markham, sponsored the breakfast at The Del; Baja California Governor Luis E. Torres was also in attendance. When Harrison left Coronado, he received a send-off at the ferry slip, serenaded by the Coronado Band, which a local newspaper reported could "vie with any band in the country in discoursing good music."

William H. Taft (1909-1913): President William Taft had a sister living in Coronado, whom he visited in April 1900, before becoming president. In 1915, after his presidency, Taft stayed at The Del—all 6 feet and 300 pounds of him—probably to attend the Panama-California Exposition.

Franklin D. Roosevelt (1932-1945): President Franklin Roosevelt stayed at the Hotel Del Coronado on October 1, 1935, for San Diego's California Pacific International Exposition. During his stay, Roosevelt flew the presidential flag, which made the hotel the official White House for the period he was in residence. The next day, Roosevelt gave a speech to 50,000 gathered in San Diego. Regarding his Hotel Del Coronado visit, a local newspaper reported, "The chief executive enjoyed an inspiring view of the broad Pacific, where a goodly part of the United States fleet rode at anchor, the lights from the warships shedding their glow over the temporary White House."

Roosevelt had close ties to Coronado because his son John was stationed here during World War II, and both President and Mrs. Roosevelt were frequent guests at The Del.

Lyndon B. Johnson (1963-1969): President Lyndon Johnson attended President Nixon's 1970 state dinner for Mexican President Gustavo Diaz Ordaz.

Richard M. Nixon (1969-1974): President Richard Nixon hosted a state dinner in the hotel's historic Crown Room for Mexican President Gustavo Diaz Ordaz on September 3, 1970. Among the 1,000 people in attendance were former President and Mrs. Lyndon Johnson and Governor and Mrs. Ronald Reagan. Aside from political luminaries, Hollywood celebrities such as Frank Sinatra and John Wayne also attended the dinner.

Gerald R. Ford (1974-1977): President Gerald Ford attended an economic conference at The Del in April 1975. He made other visits to the hotel in 1980, 1991, 1992, and 1993.

Jimmy Carter (1977-1981): When President Jimmy Carter attended the AFL-CIO Building and Construction Trades convention, a reception was given in his honor at The Del on October 11, 1979. Carter also stayed here in October 1989 in conjunction with the Habitat for Humanity project.

Ronald Reagan (1981-1989): In 1970, then California Governor Ronald Reagan attended President Nixon's state dinner. Reagan returned to The Del on October 8, 1982, when he hosted talks with Mexican president-elect Miguel de la Madrid in a private suite, which has since become known as the "Summit Suite." The hotel's "Governor's Suite" is also named in Reagan's honor, who, along with his family, were frequent guests at The Del before and during his presidency.

George Bush (1989-1993): An avid tennis player, President George Bush stayed at the Hotel Del Coronado both before and during his presidency.

Bill Clinton (1993-2001): Although President Dwight D. Eisenhower was the first president to land at Coronado's North Island Naval Air Station, President Clinton (aboard Air Force One) used the airfield many times for numerous visits to the Hotel Del Coronado during his presidency.

Laura Bush, wife of President George W. Bush, has been the hotel's most recent presidential guest (March 2001).

Adlai Ewing Stevenson (who served during Grover Cleveland's second presidency). Stevenson visited The Del in 1893 and had his hair cut in the hotel's barbershop. Vincent Surr, a bootblack, who during Stevenson's visit "was occupied by the lower extremities of a senator or two," had only vague memories of Mr. Stevenson. "My recollections of the great man are rather mixed and consist principally of a figure swathed in a barber's sheet, from which some kind of a head emerged." Surr had a clearer view of Stevenson's private secretary or valet, "What made him a conspicuous figure was his remarkable likeness to Uncle Sam, as depicted in the comic papers." More than 50 years later, Adlai Ewing Stevenson II (grandson of the first Adlai Ewing Stevenson) visited The Del in 1952.

Spiro Agnew, Hubert Humphrey, Walter Mondale, and Dan Quayle, as well as Tipper Gore, wife of Vice President Gore, Julie Nixon and David Eisenhower, Steve Ford, Ulysses S. Grant, Jr., Robert Todd Lincoln, and James Roosevelt are among other visiting dignitaries.

Movies and Movie Stars

The movie, *Some Like it Hot,* was shot on location in 1958 at the Hotel Del Coronado. The Del's spectacular Victorian architecture made a perfect backdrop for the film's 1929 setting, sharing the billing with Marilyn Monroe, Jack Lemmon, and Tony Curtis. Her husband, esteemed playwright Arthur Miller, accompanied Marilyn Monroe. Tony Curtis' wife, Janet Leigh, and their daughter (Leigh was pregnant with Jamie Lee Curtis at the time) were also on hand, as was Jack Lemmon's wife, Felicia Farr.

George Raft, who played gangster Spats Colombo in the movie *Scarface,* also visited the Del in 1936 during the filming of *Yours for the*

Asking. Other famous names include Don Ameche, Lana Turner, Joan Bennett, Darryl Zanuck, Ira Copley, and Mr. and Mrs. William Vanderbilt.

American Authors

Joseph Pulitzer (visited 1888, 1890). Joseph Pulitzer was one of the Del's very first visitors. During his 1890 visit to The Del, the *Coronado Journal* referred to him as "the most distinguished American journalist." Through his will, Joseph Pulitzer endowed the Columbia School of Journalism and established the Pulitzer Prize.

William Gillette (visited 1898). Born in 1855, actor/author William Gillette wrote the play Sherlock Holmes while staying at The Del. Gillette, who was educated at Yale and MIT, counted Mark Twain as a family friend. In 1898, Gillette approached *Sherlock Holmes'* writer Conan Doyle to obtain rights to the character. Doyle is said to have responded with, "Marry him, murder him, do anything you please with him." With rights in hand, Gillette settled into the Hotel Del Coronado where he remained four weeks writing his new play; which made him a rich man.

L. Frank Baum (visited 1904, 1905, 1907, 1908, 1909, and 1910). Perhaps the author most associated with The Del is L. Frank Baum, the creator of the Wizard of Oz series. Baum was so enamored of the hotel that he couldn't conceive of anyone not loving The Del, which he compared to Heaven itself.

Edgar Rice Burroughs (visited 1930). American writer Edgar Rice Burroughs, who wrote *Tarzan of the Apes* along with 23 other books in the Tarzan series, died in 1949. But, not before his Tarzan character had been immortalized in comic strips, television shows, and movies.

Arthur Miller (visited 1958). Referred to as the "toast of New York's literary society," Miller became famous as a result of two plays: *All My Sons* and *Death of a Salesman*. Miller divorced his wife of sixteen years and married actress Marilyn Monroe. He accompanied her to The Del for the entire filming of *Some Like it Hot*. Miller wrote the 1961 movie *The Misfits* for Monroe, which was her last starring role. After Monroe's death in 1962, Miller detailed the darker side of their marriage in his 1964 work, *After the Fall*, generating a lot of criticism for the way in which he exposed his life with Monroe.

Ray Bradbury (visited since the mid-1960s). Writer Ray Bradbury—known best for his science fiction novels such as Fahrenheit 451 and The Martian Chronicles—went public with his unabashed enthusiasm for The Del in a 1995 magazine article. He and his family started spending summers at The Del over thirty years ago.

Richard Matheson (visited 1970s). Richard Matheson wrote the 1975 Del-based novel, *Bid Time Return*. It is the story of a man who visits The Del and falls in love with a beautiful young woman featured in an old painting. Ultimately, he is able to go back in time to the year 1896, meet the beautiful woman in the portrait—who was also a guest at the hotel—and fall in love. In 1980, the book was made into a movie titled *Somewhere in Time*, starring Christopher Reeve and Jane Seymour.

Tennessee Williams (visited 1976). Playwright Tennessee Williams wrote *The Glass Menagerie, A Streetcar Named Desire*, and *Cat on a Hot Tin Roof*; the last two of which won Pulitzer Prizes. Williams was photographed at the hotel in 1976, just a few years before his death in 1983.

More recent writers who have visited The Del include Erma Bombeck, Dr. Seuss, Louis L'Amour, Truman Capote, Norman Mailer, and even the creator of "Snoopy," Charles Schultz.

CHAPTER 7
Amityville *Horror or Hoax?*

Let's take a look at this Classic Case!
This story is courtesy of Troy Taylor—visit his website for more
"spooky" stories and books at http://www.prairieghosts.com
Thanks, Troy!

There seems to be little doubt that one of the most famous American hauntings to ever be documented occurred in the quite town of Amityville, New York, a peaceful enclave on Long Island's south shore.

There stands no other case from the latter part of the 20th Century that so captured the imagination of the general public...and no other case that filled us with such fear!

I was barely a teenager when the sensational book by Jay Anson, "The Amityville Horror," was released. I will never forget snatching up a copy from a local bookstore, only to read it and then re-read it again. Could such things really happen? Could ghosts destroy a family the way that evil spirits did George and Kathy Lutz? Could a ghost force someone to kill, as demonic entities caused Ronald DeFeo to murder his entire family?

And most terrifying of all…could the American public be so easily deceived into believing the events chronicled in the book were actually real?

The answer to that question is a resounding "yes" as is proven by the fact that many people still believe in the reality of "The Amityville Horror," one of the greatest paranormal hoaxes of all time!

But how did it all begin? How could we all be fooled so easily? And what events led up to the release of the book?

To answer those inquiries, we have to go back to November 1974 and understand the true events that occurred in the house on Ocean Avenue.

The horrific carnage that prefaced the story of the "Amityville Horror" began one dark fall night in 1974. The DeFeos; Ronald Sr. and Louise, their two young sons, Mark and John, and two daughters, Dawn and Allison, were sleeping peacefully in their comfortable, three-story, Dutch Colonial home in Amityville.

The silence of the house was shattered when Ronald DeFeo murdered his parents and his siblings with a high-powered rifle. One by one, he killed each of them as they slept, although strangely, the sound of the gunshots never awakened the other family members.

DeFeo blamed the massacre on the malevolent force of an evil spirit that was present in the house. He stated that the creature began speaking to him and controlled him while he committed the murders.

Not surprisingly, he pleaded insanity at his trial. The prosecutor countered the plea by stating that DeFeo was not crazy at all, but merely trying to cash in on his parent's substantial life insurance polices.

Again though, we are left with an unanswered question…how DeFeo could have thought that he would get away with the murders and in turn, collect on the insurance policies.

Regardless, the jury ignored DeFeo's claims and found him guilty of six counts of first-degree murder. He was sentenced to 150 years in prison.

The tragedy in Amityville made grim local news but few outside of New York ever heard about the house until some time later.

The horrendous events that followed began on December 18, 1975, when a young couple named George and Kathy Lutz bought the house on Ocean Avenue for $80,000. Just a week before Christmas, they moved into their new "dream home" with Kathy's three children from a previous marriage. They would later claim that the "dream home" soon became a nightmare!

Almost from the moment that they moved into the house, the Lutz family would insist they noticed an unearthly presence in the place. They began to hear mysterious noises that they could not account for. Locked windows and doors would inexplicably open and close, as if by invisible hands.

George Lutz, a sturdy former Marine, claimed to be plagued by the sound of a phantom brass band that would march back and forth through the house. When a Catholic priest entered the house, after agreeing to exorcize it, an eerie, disembodied voice told him to "get out!"

After the aborted exorcism, the events began to intensify. The thumping and scratching sounds grew worse, a devilish creature was seen outside the windows at night, George Lutz was seemingly "possessed" by an evil spirit and green slime even oozed from the walls and ceiling. The family was further terrified by ghostly apparitions of hooded figures, clouds of flies that appeared from nowhere, cold chills, personality changes, sickly odors, objects moving about on their own, and the repeated disconnection of their telephone service.

The youngest Lutz child seemed to be in communication with a devilish pig that she called "Jodie." Kathy Lutz reported that she was often beaten and scratched by unseen hands and that one night, she was literally levitated up off the bed.

The family managed to hold out for 28 days before they gathered up their possessions and fled from the house.

According to their story, they left so quickly that they didn't take their furniture or many of their other possessions with them. The demonic spirits, they said, had driven them from their home!

And then, things really started to get scary...

In February 1976, not long after the Lutz family left the house, local residents were stunned to see a news team doing a live news feed from the house on Ocean Avenue.

The news crew filmed a séance and a dramatic investigation, conducted by two of America's most famous "demonologists." The Amityville house would soon become the center of a three-ring circus!

The investigators went to the house for the first time in February and while supposedly George Lutz refused to accompany them, he did loan them a key.

They stated that they found old newspapers around the house and that the refrigerator was still stocked with food. It was obvious to them that the Lutz family had left in a hurry.

Two other psychics were brought to the house to conduct their séance. They later reported that they "sensed" an "unearthly presence" in the house and one of the investigators claimed to experience heart palpitations that he blamed on the occult forces.

The house was haunted, they said, by the angry spirits of Indians who had once inhabited the area and by "inhuman spirits." The story was that the Shinnecock Indians had used that very parcel of land as a place where sick and insane members of the tribe were isolated until they died. They did not bury the dead there however because they supposedly believed the land was "infested with demons."

Not long after, George and Kathy Lutz teamed up with a writer named Jay Anson and together, they authored what would become a best-selling book called *The Amityville Horror*.

The book went on to spawn the movie and several sequels. The lead paranormal investigators were hired by the producer and the production company to serve as consultants about the supernatural occurrences portrayed in the film. They also made the rounds of the talk show circuit, discussing the horrifying events in Amityville.

The "Amityville Horror" grew from news reports and newspaper articles to books, magazines, and television. The story would become internationally known and around the world, people recognized the name of Amityville. Most amazing, was the fact that this terrifying story was absolutely true...or so it read in bold print on the cover of the phenomenally selling book.

But not everyone was convinced, even in paranormal circles. In fact, a few of them smelled something bad in Amityville!

In 1976, George Lutz was approached by a paranormal investigator from New York. He received the phone call from Lutz on February 16, and wanted the house to be investigated.

Lutz asked about a fee for the group's services and was told that they did not charge for the investigation but that if the story was a hoax, the public would know.

A few days later, Lutz called and cancelled the investigation. He claimed that he and his wife did not want any publicity about the house. This may have been why the television news story came as such a surprise a few days later!

As the story of the "Amityville Horror" was becoming an international sensation, the investigator from New York was at work collecting evidence and materials about the house and the claims made by the Lutz family, the author of the book, and the media.

Although convinced of the validity of the paranormal and supernatural activity, he was not convinced of the truth behind the Amityville case. While it was possible that a haunting could have occurred at the house, especially in light of the violent events that had taken place, there was something not quite right about the accounts of the Lutz's. After some initial investigation, he became sure that a hoax was being perpetrated on the public and such a hoax could prove to be damaging for legitimate paranormal cases in the future. With that in mind, he became determined to show that the entire story was a farce. Little did he know that he would face an uphill battle.

The general public had been so force-fed the story by the media that the evidence against the house being haunted seemed to fall on deaf ears. Thanks to the fact that the truth was not as glamorous or as dramatic as the original story, the new story was scarcely reported and was barely noticed at first.

In fact, diaries of the investigations were turned into a book that did not get published for many years after the events took place. The problem remained that the public loved the story and the house on Ocean Avenue became a Long Island landmark.

People traveled from all over the country to drive past and stare at it. Tourists made it their first stop on Long Island and locals soon began calling the sightseers the "Amityville Horribles." The trouble with curiosity seekers and complaints from locals were so bad in the late 1970s that they drove one Amityville police chief into early retirement!

The investigator had discovered that the "Amityville Horror" was pure invention. In 1979, a lawyer confessed to his part in the hoax during a paranormal radio show. This lawyer had been the lawyer for convicted killer Ronald DeFeo and he admitted that he and George Lutz had concocted the story of the haunting over a few bottles of wine.

The motive was to get a new trial for DeFeo, using a "Devil made him do it" defense. According to the lawyer, Lutz merely wanted to get out from under a mortgage that he couldn't afford. His business was in trouble and he needed a scheme to bail him out.

The investigator from New York found ample proof, outside of the glaring confession, that the story was a hoax. He gained access to the house on many occasions and found that the so-called "Red Room," where the book claimed occult ceremonies took place, was nothing more than a small pipe well that gave access to them if they needed to be repaired. No "demonic face" had ever appeared on the bricks inside of the fireplace. He also noted that the original front door of the house (blown off its hinges in the book) was still in place and intact.

In addition, he found a writer for the local newspaper that had also been suspicious of the story. After some searching, the columnist discovered that the Lutz's had returned the day after "fleeing" from the house to hold a garage sale. He also charged that during their "28-day nightmare" that they never once called the police for assistance, something that would have been commonly done under the circumstances. The list of things that did not happen in the house went on and on and the evidence for an "Amityville Hoax" was overwhelming.

To the general public, the truth remains much more of a shadowy thing and some theorists who believe that there are still things about the story that do not add up will point to a string of tragedies that surround the case.

The writer who penned the original story for newspapers and for *Good Housekeeping* magazine, died a few years after the story broke under mysterious circumstances.

The author of the best-selling book made a fortune from the story but died shortly after he received his first million dollar advance for his next book. That book, an occult novel entitled 666, was a failure.

The Demonologist suffered a heart attack a few years after his initial investigations of Amityville. He maintained the illness was caused by the house.

The son of the house's new owners died an early, tragic death. He used the bedroom that had once belonged to Ronald DeFeo for several years.

The investigator, who took on the hoaxers, almost died from a major heart attack in 1976 and then passed away several years later. His death was untimely and cut short a distinguished career. He would not live to see his book on the case published.

Some would say that the house "got them" but others would admit that these events are nothing more than strange coincidences that have been arranged to look like something they most likely are not.

To this author, they are a perfect example of this entire case as a whole...a blending of fact with fiction in an attempt to titillate and terrify the American public.

Sources:
The Amityville Horror by Jay Anson (1977)
The Amityville Horror Conspiracy by Dr. Stephen Kaplan (1995)
ESP, Hauntings and Poltergeists by Loyd Auerbach (1986)

The Encyclopedia of Ghosts and Spirits by Rosemary Ellen Guiley (2000)

True Tales of the Unknown: Beyond Reality by Sharon Jarvis (1991)

The Encyclopedia of Ghosts by Daniel Cohen (1984)

CHAPTER 8
The Myrtles Plantation
"One of America's Most Haunted Homes"

7747 U.S. Highway 61, P.O. Box 1100
St. Francisville, Louisiana 70775
John & Teeta LeBleu Moss, Proprietors
Phone: 225-635-6277 Fax: 225-635-5837 Email:
myrtles@bsf.net

The Myrtles Plantation, circa 1796, invites you to step into the past to experience antebellum splendor. You will see fine antiques and architectural treasures of the South and discover why The Myrtles has been called one of "America's Most Haunted Homes."

The Myrtles has been featured in *New York Times, Forbes, Gourmet, Veranda, Travel and Leisure, Country Inns, Colonial Homes, Delta SKY, the Oprah Show, A & E, The History Channel, The Travel Channel, The Learning Channel, National Geographic Explorer, Good Morning America,* and *The Haunting of Louisiana.*

Legend says that a slave woman, named Chloe, was owned by the Woodruffe family and was the judge's mistress and Chloe wanted to keep that position.

Eventually, the judge seemed to tire of Chloe and she feared what might become of her so she took to listening at keyholes in order to learn her possible fate. The judge caught her one day and had her ear lobe cut off for punishment! Because of that, Chloe always wore a turban.

Eventually, Chloe devised a plan for insuring her place in the household. In a birthday cake, made for one of the Woodruffe's daughters, Chloe added a small amount of poison from an oleander plant. This was to sicken the daughters and their mother to the point that she could nurse them back to health and appear to be the hero. The plan backfired though, and the mother and children died.

As the story goes…the other slaves, perhaps frightened that their owner would punish them, dragged Chloe from her room and hanged her from a nearby tree. Her body was later cut down, weighted with rocks, and thrown into the Mississippi River.

Chloe still wanders the house and grounds of the Myrtles Plantation. She sometimes shows up in photos. The Woodruffe children are more often heard playing and laughing.

Be sure to watch:

Unsolved Mysteries filmed an episode at the Myrtles Plantation late April, early May.

In addition, *the Travel Channel* filmed scenes at the Myrtles Plantation to be aired sometime in October.

Fox Family Channel, Unsolved Mysteries, Discovery Channel, and the Travel Channel for upcoming features on the Myrtles Plantation, one of America's most haunted homes…

Strange Things…seem to abound at the Myrtles
In 1927 a man was killed during a robbery of the plantation. It has been said that his ghost roams the property and orders strangers to leave.

The Woodruffe children have been seen and heard on the property, laughing and playing. They have even been spotted perched in the chandeliers or peering at guests from the foot of their beds.

Sometimes images of the children show up in a hallway mirror. People often hear their names called from different rooms only to find they are alone in the house.

Visitors and guests often photograph Mryt, the house cat. The 14-year-old black cat poses dutifully, but sometimes does not appear in the pictures. The surroundings will be there, or the person petting the cat will appear in the photo but the cat won't. There will only be a puff of smoke or a blank space. No one can seem to explain it.

Startled visitors to the Myrtles have reported seeing a Voodoo priestess, chanting over a little girl.

Even odder still, some have seen a ballet dancer, complete with black tutu, who dances about a foot off the ground.

Some folks have reported seeing a body, from the waist up, floating in midair.

The grand piano has been known to play by itself.

People have heard crying babies.

Others report the sound of a man staggering up the stairs in the dead of night and collapsing on the 17th stair. (This has been attributed to the ghost of William Winter, who staggered up the stairs as he was dying of a gunshot wound in 1871, and collapsed into his wife's arms on the 17th step.)

Experiences of the Owners

Plantation owners John and Teeta Moss take advantage of the homes' spiritual past by offering a "Mystery Tour" on Friday and Saturday nights. The tour highlights some of the stories and pinpoints the history of the happenings over the years.

Shortly after buying and moving into the home, Moss had her own encounter with one of the disembodied spirits roaming the grounds.

When they first moved into the house, her son was lying in bed one night and told her he saw a young girl on the chandelier.

Moss said her son was adamant he was seeing a young girl above him. The young boy said the apparition wore a white dress and had yellow or blonde hair.

As she talked to her son, Moss thought it might have been the imagination of a two-year-old running wild. However, she later talked to a psychologist friend who told her that while children at that age can describe things they see, they cannot conjure images and describe them.

In another instance, at ten months old, Moss' son was asleep in a king-sized bed in an upstairs bedroom. She was taking care of some work on the computer. As she worked, a nagging feeling to check on her son came over her. As she was walking back to the house, she spotted the young boy toddling toward a pond in the back yard. He had descended the stairs and made it outside without any assistance.

As she screamed to the boy, Moss felt the feeling of a warm blanket being wrapped around her.

"It told me that we would be alright," Moss said. "As long as we were in this house, nothing would happen to my family."

CHAPTER 9
The Winchester Mystery House

525 South Winchester Boulevard
San Jose, CA 95128
Ph: (408) 247-2101 Fax: 408-985-7913

I am a big Stephen King fan. One of my favorite movies is Rose Red, about the house that keeps growing and growing...

The story was based on the history of The Winchester Mystery House, although the movie was filmed elsewhere. The information was taken from their website, with permission to share with you.

A Little Background

In 1884, a wealthy widow, named Sarah L. Winchester, began a construction project of such magnitude that it was to occupy the lives of carpenters and craftsmen until her death thirty-eight years later.

The Victorian mansion, designed and built by the Winchester Rifle heiress, is filled with so many unexplained oddities that it has come to be known as the Winchester Mystery House. Unlike most homes of its era, this 160-room Victorian mansion has modern heating and sewer systems, gaslights that operate by pressing a button, three working elevators, and 47 fireplaces. From rambling roofs and exquisite hand inlaid parquet floors to the gold and silver chandeliers and Tiffany art glass windows, you will be impressed by the staggering amount of creativity, energy, and expense poured into each and every detail.

Just the Facts…

Number of rooms: 160
Cost: $5,500,000
Date of Construction: 1884 – September 5, 1922 (38 continuous years!)
Number of stories: Prior to 1906 Earthquake- 7; presently 4
Number of acres: Originally 161.919; presently 4
Number of basements: 2
Heating: Steam, forced air, fireplaces
Number of windows: Frames 1,257; panes approx. 10,000
Number of doors: Doorways 467, doors approx. 950; not including cabinet doors.
Number of fireplaces: 47 (gas, wood, or coal burning)
Number of chimneys: Presently 17, with evidence of 2 others
Number of cars at her death: 2 (a 1917 Pierce Arrow Limousine & a 1916 4 cylinder Buick truck)
Number of bedrooms: Approximately 40
Number of kitchens: 5 or 6
Number of staircases: 40, total of stair steps- 367
Number of skylights: Approximately 52
Number of gallons of paint required to paint entire home: Over 20,000
Number of ballrooms: 2 (one nearly complete, and one under construction)
Blueprints available: No, Mrs. Winchester never had a master set of blueprints, but did sketch out individual rooms on paper and even tablecloth.

Tour through 110 of the 160 rooms and look for the bizarre phenomena that gave the mansion its name; a window built into the floor, staircases leading to nowhere, a chimney that rises four floors, doors that open onto blank walls, and upside down posts!

No one has been able to explain the mysteries that exist within the Winchester Mansion or why Sarah Winchester kept the carpenters' hammers pounding 24 hours a day for 38 years.

It is believed that after the untimely deaths of her baby daughter and husband, son of the Winchester Rifle manufacturer, Mrs. Winchester was convinced by a medium that continuous building would appease the evil spirits of those killed by the famous "Gun that Won the West" and help her attain eternal life. Certainly, her $20,000,000 inheritance was sufficient to support her obsession until her death at 82!

The largest cabinet in the mansion goes straight through to the back thirty rooms of the mansion.

The Garden Tour...

A visit to the Winchester Mystery House is not complete until you have strolled through the beautiful Victorian gardens that surround it. Great care has been taken to restore the grounds to that time when Sarah Winchester had a full-time staff of eight gardeners, imported trees, shrubs, and flowers from all parts of the world.

Nearly 14,000 miniature boxwood hedges, large flowering Carolina cherry laurels, plants, and flowers have been replanted to provide beautiful color year-round. Numerous handcrafted European lead statues and elaborate fountains have been restored.

You will see the original mythological statues including Mother Nature, Cupid, a cherub, hippocampus, American Indian, deer, egret, frogs, and swans. Mrs. Winchester's fascination with the supernatural is evident in the gardens, where you can count thirteen California Fan Palms lining the front driveway!

The self-guided Garden Tour includes a guide map and narrative tapes at the 10 major points of interest. Guests also see the green house, garage, car wash, pump, and tank houses. Wheel chaired guests are invited to tour the Gardens and Historic Firearms Museum as our guests and at no charge (unfortunately the Mansion Tour is NOT accessible to wheel chairs or infant strollers.)

The daisy was Mrs. Winchester's favorite flower, and she used it often including a custom-made stained glass window on the second floor, which looks out onto the front lawn.

Behind the Scenes Tour...

The Behind-the-Scenes Tour is a guided tour which takes guests into areas which had been unexplored for over seventy-five years. On tour, you will learn how Mrs. Winchester's 160-acre estate functioned. You will go into the stables, dehydrator, plumber's workshop, the unfinished ballroom, and one of the basements.

You will also learn about Victorian architecture as your guide points out the many features used in the building of the Winchester mansion. Safety hats will be worn on the tour. The Behind-the-Scenes Tour is limited to those ten years and older. Sorry, due to safety concerns, children nine years old and under and babies are not permitted.

The Winchester Firearms Museum

The "Gun that Won the West" is the main attraction in the Firearms Museum, one of the largest Winchester Rifle collections on the West Coast.

See the collection of guns that preceded the famous Winchester Rifle, including B. Tyler Henry's 1860 repeating rifle that Oliver Winchester adapted and improved upon to produce his first repeating rifle, the Winchester Model 1866.

Learn about the Model 1873, which came to be called the "Gun that Won the West." See a collection of the Limited Edition Winchester Commemorative Rifles including the Centennial '66, the Theodore Roosevelt, and the renowned John Wayne.

The Winchester Antique Products Museum

This museum contains a rare collection of antique products once manufactured by the Winchester Products Company, a subsidiary of the Winchester Repeating Arms Company. In the years following World War I, the parent company launched a Post-war Program, aimed at expanding the manufacture of new products in order to fill the factory space previously used for military production.

At one time, there were 6,300 individually owned Winchester stores carrying these products, which made it the largest hardware chain store organization in the world!

The museum now displays items produced in the 1920s ranging from Winchester cutlery, flashlights, lawn-mowers, boy's wagons, fishing tackle and roller skates, to food choppers, electric irons, and farm and garden tools.

The following article is an overview of the Winchester Mansion Story, courtesy of Troy Taylor. To visit Troy's site, go here: https://www.prairieghosts.com/president.html
Thanks, Troy

Our story begins in September 1839 with the birth of a baby girl to Leonard and Sarah Pardee of New Haven, Connecticut.

The baby's name was also Sarah and as she reached maturity, she became the belle of the city. She was well-received at all social events, thanks to her musical skills, her fluency in various foreign languages and her sparkling charm. Her beauty was also well known by the young men about town, despite her diminutive size. Although she was petite and stood only four feet, ten inches, she made up for this in personality and loveliness.

At the same time that Sarah was growing up, a young man was also maturing in another prominent New Haven family. The young man's name was William Wirt Winchester and he was the son of Oliver Winchester, a shirt manufacturer and businessman.

In 1857, he took over the assets of a firm, which made the Volcanic Repeater, a rifle that used a lever mechanism to load bullets into the breech.

Obviously, this type of gun was a vast improvement over the muzzle-loading rifles of recent times, but Winchester still saw room for advance.

In 1860, the company developed the Henry Rifle, which had a tubular magazine located under the barrel. Because it was easy to reload and could fire rapidly, the Henry was said to average one shot every three seconds. It became the first true repeating rifle and a favorite among the Northern troops at the outbreak of the Civil War.

Money began to pour in and Oliver Winchester soon amassed a large fortune from government contracts and private sales. He re-organized the company and changed the name to the Winchester Repeating Arms Company.

The family prospered and on September 30, 1862, at the height of the Civil War, William Wirt Winchester and Sarah Pardee were married in an elaborate ceremony in New Haven.

Four years later, on July 15, 1866, Sarah gave birth to a daughter named Annie Pardee Winchester. Just a short time later, the first disaster struck for Sarah, as her daughter contracted an illness known as "marasmus," a children's disease in which the body wastes away. The infant died on July 24.

Sarah was so shattered by this event that she withdrew into herself and teetered on the edge of madness for some time. In the end, it would be nearly a decade before she returned to her normal self but she and William would never have a another child.

Not long after Sarah returned to her family and home, another tragedy struck. William, now heir to the Winchester empire, was struck down with pulmonary tuberculosis. He died on March 7, 1881.

As a result of his death, Sarah inherited over $20 million dollars, an incredible sum, especially in those days. She also received 48.9 percent of the Winchester Repeating Arms Company and an income of about $1000 per day, which was not taxable until 1913.

But her newfound wealth could do nothing to ease her pain. Sarah grieved deeply, not only for her husband, but also for her lost child. A short time later, a friend suggested that Sarah might speak to a Spiritualist medium about her loss.

"Your husband is here," the medium told her and then went on to provide a description of William Winchester. "He says for me to tell you that there is a curse on your family, which took the life of him and your child. It will soon take you too. A curse has resulted from the terrible weapon created by the Winchester family. Thousands of persons have died because of it and their spirits are now seeking vengeance."

Sarah was then told that she must sell her property in New Haven and head towards the setting sun. She would be guided by her husband and when she found her new home in the west, she would recognize it.

"You must start a new life," said the medium, "and build a home for yourself and for the spirits who have fallen from this terrible weapon too. You can never stop building the house. If you continue building, you will live. Stop and you will die."

Shortly after the séance, Sarah sold her home in New Haven and with a vast fortune at her disposal, moved west to California. She believed that she was guided by the hand of her dead husband and she did not stop traveling until she reached the Santa Clara Valley in 1884. Here, she found a six-room home under construction, which belonged to a Dr. Caldwell. She entered into negotiations with him and soon convinced him to sell her the house and the 162 acres, which it rested on.

She tossed away any previous plans for the house and started building whatever she chose to. She had her pick of local workers and craftsmen and for the next 36 years, they built and rebuilt, altered and changed and constructed and demolished one section of the house after another. She kept 22 carpenters at work, year around, 24 hours each day. The sounds of hammers and saws sounded throughout the day and night.

As the house grew to include 26 rooms, railroad cars were switched onto a nearby line to bring building materials and imported furnishings to the house. The house was rapidly growing and expanding and while Sarah claimed to have no master plan for the structure, she met each morning with her foreman and they would go over her hand-sketched plans for the day's work.

The plans were often chaotic but showed a real flair for building. Sometimes though, they would not work out the right way, but Sarah always had a quick solution. If this happened, they would just build another room around an existing one.

As the days, weeks and months passed, the house continued to grow. Rooms were added to rooms and then turned into entire wings, doors were joined to windows, levels turned into towers and peaks, and the place eventually grew to a height of seven stories.

Inside of the house, three elevators were installed, as were 47 fireplaces.

There were countless staircases which led nowhere; a blind chimney that stops short of the ceiling, closets that opened to blank walls, trap doors, double-back hallways, skylights that were located one above another, doors that opened to steep drops to the lawn below, and dozens of other oddities. Even all of the stair posts were installed upside-down and many of the bathrooms had glass doors on them.

It was also obvious that Sarah was intrigued by the number "13." Nearly all of the windows contained 13 panes of glass; the walls had 13 panels, the greenhouse had 13 cupolas, many of the wooden floors contained 13 sections, some of the rooms had 13 windows, and every staircase but one had 13 steps.

This exception is unique in its own right…it is a winding staircase with 42 steps, which would normally be enough to take a climber up three stories. In this case, however, the steps only rise nine feet because each step is only two inches high.

While all of this seems like madness to us, it all made sense to Sarah. In this way, she could control the spirits who came to the house for evil purposes, or who were outlaws or vengeful people in their past life. These bad men, killed by Winchester rifles, could wreak havoc on Sarah's life. The house had been designed into a maze to confuse and discourage the bad spirits.

The house continued to grow and by 1906, it had reached a towering seven stories tall. Sarah continued her occupancy, and expansion, of the house, living in melancholy solitude with no one other than her servants, the workmen and, of course, the spirits. It was said that on sleepless nights, when she was not communing with the spirit world about the designs for the house, Sarah would play her grand piano into the early hours of the morning. According to legend, the piano would be admired by passers-by on the street outside, despite the fact that two of the keys were badly out of tune.

The most tragic event occurred within the house when the great San Francisco Earthquake of 1906 struck. When it was all over, portions of the Winchester Mansion were nearly in ruins. The top three floors of the house had collapsed into the gardens and would never be rebuilt. In addition, the fireplace that was located in the Daisy Room (where Mrs. Winchester was sleeping on the night of the earthquake) collapsed, shifting the room and trapping Sarah inside.

She became convinced that the earthquake had been a sign from the spirits who were furious that she had nearly completed the house. In order to insure that the house would never be finished, she decided to board up the front 30 rooms of the mansion so that the construction would not be complete—and also so that the spirits who fell when portions of the house collapsed would be trapped inside forever.

For the next several months, the workmen toiled to repair the damage done by the earthquake, although actually the mammoth structure had fared far better than most of the buildings in the area. Only a few of the rooms had been badly harmed, although it had lost the highest floors and several cupolas and towers had toppled over.

The expansion on the house began once more. The number of bedrooms increased from 15 to 20 and then to 25. Chimneys were installed all over the place, although strangely, they served no purpose. Some believe that perhaps they were added because the old stories say that ghosts like to appear and disappear through them.

On a related note, it has also been documented that only two mirrors were installed in the house....Sarah believed that ghosts were afraid of their own reflection.

On September 4, 1922, after a conference session with the spirits in the séance room, Sarah went to her bedroom for the night. At some point in the early morning hours, she died in her sleep at the age of 83.

She left all of her possessions to her niece, Frances Marriot, who had been handling most of Sarah's business affairs for some time. Little did anyone know, but by this time, Sarah's large bank account had dwindled considerably. Rumor had it that somewhere in the house was hidden a safe containing a fortune in jewelry and a solid-gold dinner service with which Sarah had entertained her ghostly guests. Her relatives forced open a number of safes but found only old fish lines, socks, newspaper clippings about her daughter's and her husband's deaths, a lock of baby hair, and a suit of woolen underwear. No solid gold dinner service was ever discovered.

The furnishings, personal belongings, surplus construction, and decorative materials were removed from the house and the structure itself was sold to a group of investors who planned to use it as a tourist attraction.

One of the first to see the place when it opened to the public was Robert L. Ripley, who featured the house in his popular column, "Believe it or Not." The house was initially advertised as being 148 rooms, but so confusing was the floor plan that every time a room count was taken, a different total came up. The place was so puzzling that it was said that the workmen took more than six weeks just to get the furniture out of it. The moving men became so lost because it was a "labyrinth", they told the magazine, American Weekly, in 1928 that it was a house "where downstairs leads neither to the cellar nor upstairs to the roof."

The rooms of the house were counted over and over again and five years later, it was estimated that 160 rooms existed...although no one is really sure if even that is correct.

Today, the house has been declared a California Historical Landmark and is registered with the National Park Service as "a large, odd dwelling with an unknown number of rooms."

Most would say that such a place must still harbor at least a few of the ghosts who came to reside there at the invitation of Sarah Winchester. The question is though; do they really haunt the place? Some would say that perhaps no ghosts ever walked there at all...that the Winchester mansion is nothing more than the product of an eccentric woman's mind and too much wealth being allowed into the wrong hands.

There is no question that we can regard the place as one of the world's "largest haunted houses," based on nothing more than the legend of the place alone. Is this a case where we need to draw the line between what is a real haunted spot...and what is a really great story?

Is the Winchester Mansion really haunted? You will have to decide that for yourself, although some people have already made up their minds.

There have been a number of strange events reported at the Winchester House for many years and they continue to be reported today.

Dozens of psychics have visited the house over the years and most have come away convinced, or claim to be convinced, that spirits still wander the place. In addition to the ghost of Sarah Winchester, there have also been many other sightings throughout the years.

In the years that the house has been open to the public, employees and visitors alike have had unusual encounters here. There have been footsteps, *banging doors, mysterious voices, windows that bang so hard they shatter, cold spots, strange moving lights, doorknobs that turn by themselves... and don't forget the scores of psychics who have their own claims of phenomena to report.*

Obviously, these are all of the standard reports of a haunted house...but are the stories merely wishful thinking? Reports of ghosts and spirits to continue the tradition of Sarah Winchester's bizarre legacy? Or could the stories be true? Was the house really built as a monument to the dead? Do phantoms still lurk in the maze-like corridors of the Winchester Mystery House?

I urge you to visit the house if you should ever get the chance. Perhaps that would be the best time to answer the questions that I have just posed to you. I can promise that you will find not another piece of American architecture like the Winchester mansion....

And who knows what else you might find while you're there?

SOURCES:

THE HAUNTING OF AMERICA by Troy Taylor (2001)

GHOSTS OF THE OLD WEST by Earl Murray (1998)

HAUNTED HOUSES by Richard Winer and Nancy Osborn (1979)

PROMINENT AMERICAN GHOSTS by Susy Smith (1967)

AMERICAN WEEKLY Magazine (April 1928)

HAUNTED HOUSES OF CALIFORNIA by Antoinette May (1990)

GHOST STALKERS GD. TO HAUNTED CALIFORNIA By Richard Senate (1998)

HAUNTED HOUSES USA by Delores Riccio and Joan Bingham (1989)

HAUNTED PLACES: THE NATIONAL DIRECTORY by Dennis William Hauck (1996)

GREAT AMERICAN MYSTERIES by Randall Floyd (1990)

ENCYCLOPEDIA OF GHOSTS AND SPIRITS by Rosemary Ellen Guiley (1992)

THE GHOSTLY REGISTER by Arthur Myers (1986)

CHAPTER 10
C. C. Cohen Restaurant and Bar

103 Market House Square
Paducah, Kentucky 42001
Phone: 270-442-6391
Alan Raidt, Owner

THE GHOST STORY

About 1850, this building was constructed to house a distillery, a grocery distributor, and a host of other businesses.

Around 1900, the Cohen family bought it to house three of their passions...a dry goods store; with the finest turn-of-the century clothing, shoes and hats...a pawn shop, where the Cohen family could turn an honest (or perhaps dishonest) dollar, and their home on the 2nd floor.

Stella was a Cohen sister. The A. Cohen Loan office did a booming business on the Market House Square. (His checks are framed around the building.) The dry goods store did well, and everything was great until...

The Cohens started dying. Stella's husband was murdered in an alley behind Cohen's so she and her sister closed up shop to live with her nine cats and two Dobermans until Stella's sister died around 1950. Stella lived upstairs, now renovated, with a meticulously rebuilt parlor, until the 1970s.

In the Early 1980s, the building sold and things started happening. Workmen on the renovation lost tools or their equipment didn't work.

Alan Raidt opened C.C. Cohen back up and still things kept happening.

"CC Cohen restaurant is my business now, has been for eight years, and Stella keeps making herself known. I hope she is happy...I am," says Alan Raidt, the owner.

Alan Raidt and Friends have been playing Saturday nights for years at C.C. Cohen's. The band plays blues, ballads, blends and some classic rock.

"Stella we mean you only the greatest respect. I've left some of my favorite antiques, antique guitars, etc., in your building. Keep them safe please."

Alan Raidt, Owner, CC Cohen Restaurant and Bar April 1996

CHAPTER 11
Napa River Inn

500 Main Street Napa, CA 94559
Tel: (877) 251-8500 Fax: (707-251-8405

Stories have abounded for years that the former Hatt Mill Building, now the site of the Napa River Inn, is haunted.

This former warehouse and feed store is currently the setting for a luxury hotel. The pressed tin wainscoting, once rusty, has been re-gilded. Fine silk and satin chairs have replaced the burlap bags, stuffed with grain.

The rooms, formerly strung with pulleys and conveyor belts, have joined the electronic age with cable television and data ports.

How would the new management respond when asked about a ghost that walks the halls at night?

Napa River Inn's General Manager, Nancy Lochmann, doesn't bat an eye. She politely inquires, "Which ghost?" It seems the Inn is visited by more than one otherworldly being, at least as reported by several self-described reliable witnesses.

Lochmann, who has worked at the hotel for five years...since its planning stages, explains the history of the first ghost. It was the son of the building's original owner, Captain Albert Hatt.

Originally, from Germany, Hatt had been a sailor since the age of fourteen. Captain Hatt married Alma (Hogan) and had six children. In 1884, he purchased the Napa River land from William Coombs and built the Hatt Building.

The building was used as a bonded warehouse with an upstairs roller-skating rink built of White Rock maple. In 1887, the silo section was built for storage and another building housed machinery for crushing and cleaning grains.

It might be difficult to imagine Napa in the mid-1800s, but the river was then a bustling focus of trade in the valley. Industrial plants lined the shores and the waterway was used to transport raw and manufactured goods as well as people.

Captain Hatt's buildings, on more than two acres with adjacent wharves, were positioned in the midst of the activity. Captain Hatt's son, Albert Jr., married Margaret (Riley) in 1889. They had five children and Margaret died in 1906.

At age 46, apparently overburdened with the responsibilities of caring for his five children, despondent at being sued over the ownership of a company steamboat and in poor health, Albert Jr., hung himself. This happened from a beam in the warehouse on April 1, 1912, in the area now occupied by Sweetie Pies Bakery.

The Ghost Stories

The first ghost sightings were visions of a woman.
The woman wears a white dress and seems to be searching for someone. It might have been Margaret, so much in love with her husband, perhaps trying to stop him from taking his life.

Lochmann said that this was the first ghost they heard about. She admits to unusual occurrences that can't be explained.

In one room, a guest complained that someone kept turning off the fireplace and the room got very cold. A visitor from UC Davis said it got so cold in his room that it felt like the air conditioning was on.

After the hotel was featured on a Travel Channel television program, *Haunted Hotels*, people wanted to stay in the scariest rooms.

Lochmann said that guests are always mentioning that they hear things.

The hotel's maintenance engineer didn't think much at first about the idea of a ghost roaming the halls He thought it was interesting and enjoyed hearing the stories.

Last year, in preparation for a celebration for the Napa River Inn being named in the National Trust of Historic Hotels, the building was decorated with many old photographs of the Hatt family. The engineer set up pictures on easels as family members were arriving. The feeling of expectation surrounding the celebration.

He was in the storeroom, cleaning the painting supplies in a deep sink. Above him were, stacked on the shelves, were plastic glassware bins. They suddenly flew off the shelves, as if someone had kicked them.

Lochmann says that maybe it's just a good excuse for the staff. Staff? Does Lochmann mean that more people have reported unusual events? Lochmann is seemingly untroubled by a specter wandering the property.

JH also has been with the hotel prior to its official opening, first as a security guard and night auditor. He is currently the senior bell captain.

JH, 62, retired from a civil service job before working for the inn, speaks in a no-nonsense manner of the period before the hotel was open for guests. He would be there by himself and the elevator would keep going up and down. The elevators can (be adjusted to) go down, but they don't go up by themselves.

More than once JH heard doors open and close, certain he'd been alone in the building. He has walked down the hall and had the hair on the back his neck stand on end.

A guest recently complained she'd put clothes in a drawer and closed it. When she turned back around, the drawer was open...this happened twice.

The guests seem quite understanding when the staff explains that a ghost may be responsible for various occurrences.

One guest wrote about her eerie experiences at an online review site, and was happy to discuss it further, as long as she was referred to as "Lilly."

Many people, who report ghosts, apparently have a tendency to shy away from publicity. She has stayed at the Inn three times.

"I heard a heavy dress sway down the hall," Lilly said in her review. "A door opened right across the hall in 208, then shut. I heard hard footsteps of what sounded like a man."

"A door at the other end of the hall, room 207, opened then closed with such a force! I heard walking down the hallway toward room 208. Room 208 is directly above Sweetie Pies, where Captain Hatt reportedly hung himself."

Sweetie Pies is a bustling place each morning. The aroma of coffee scents the air and conversation at the tables is lively. In the middle of the room, a grain-bagging machine remains as one of the last vestiges of the Hatt Mill.

The manager, CF, is good-natured about the spirit or spirits, although she hasn't experienced them for herself. She says that she has not heard any of the late night shuffling or felt any late night vibes. Although, after the *Haunted Hotel* show was on, a lot of people ask about the ghosts.

Now, the subject of the second ghost.

A reliable source relates the experience of friends who recently visited the hotel for the first time. The couple encountered a man coming down the stairway and asked him the location of the restaurant. The man said, "This is no dining establishment, this is Napa Milling and I'm the owner, Robert Keig."

After they walked past him, they noted a "distinct smell of hay and grain." When they turned around, he had vanished!

Later, they saw a photograph of Robert Keig, who purchased the Mill from Captain Hatt in 1912. They went ballistic! They said that the man in the photo was the man they encountered on the stairs that night!

Other trustworthy sources stayed the night and heard footsteps outside the door as well as machines running downstairs.

The Keig family operated the Napa Mill Feed Store until 1974. Although somewhat bemused, Keig's grandson, Paul Keig, appears open-minded about all the fuss about ghosts. Harry Price, Managing Partner of the Napa Mill Development that includes the Napa River Inn, recently gave Keig a tour of the property. This was the first time Keig, a Napa native and resident had returned to the site since his family owned the business.

Keig walked through the property and reminisced about his time there. He said that the skating rink area was where they stored grains and seeds that didn't move fast. The original skating rink, its maple floor expensively and painstakingly restored, now houses several guest rooms (including the infamous room 207 and room 208), a lobby, and the Keig Board Room.

Keig said that the new area is amazing and quite a difference. Upon inspecting the bagging machinery in Sweetie Pies, Keig declared the he bet he was the only person who knows how the machinery worked. No one disputed him.

Keig has fond memories of his grandfather. He was neat and a workaholic. Keig spent years and years working at the Mill. Did anything in the mill ever frighten him? He said that when he and his father would come down for a late grain shipment, he (being a kid) had to walk through the entire dark warehouse by himself and turn on the light switch!

He laughed at the memory. What does Keig think of the current Mill? Keig thinks that the current mill is helping downtown Napa. The downtown is turning around now.

When Lochmann mentioned the rumor that his grandfather hadn't quite departed the premises, Keig smiles and says that if you see Grandpa, tell him I said 'HI.'

CHAPTER 12
The Bullock Hotel

633 Main Street
Deadwood, SD 57732
1-800-336-1876
Bullock@HistoricBullock.com

Step back in time and walk through the very same corridors, rooms, and hallways that Deadwood's first Sheriff Seth Bullock himself still proudly haunts! Experience 19th Century history and elegance combined with 21st Century amenities. Deadwood's first and finest hotel is restored to its breath-taking Victorian decor. The Hotel offers historic deluxe accommodations, 24-hour gaming action, breakfast and brunch in Seth's Cellar, and the finest spirits in Bully's Bar. (Pun intended!)

The Bullock Hotel was Deadwood's first hotel, built in 1895 by the first sheriff of Deadwood, Seth Bullock, and his business partner Sol Star. The fire of 1894 had destroyed the two-story frame building that stood on Main. It was then determined to build the hotel up and over the large, fireproof 1876 warehouse that was still standing at the rear after withstanding two separate fires.

Native pink and white sandstone from Andrew's Quarry in Boulder Canyon was used to create the banded facade. A large tin roof pediment typical of the Victorian period graces the third floor. The style of the building is ITALIANTE and is the only such example in Deadwood. The rear building faced Whitewood Creek, where ox teams formerly unloaded at the doors, which makes the Bullock the only building in town, which has two frontages. The small building adjoining the hotel was originally the Gentlemen's Bar, where you could slake your thirst and, of course, gamble.

The Bullock boasted a restaurant that could seat 100 people comfortably and offered such delicacies as pheasant and lobster. It also had a kitchen, pantry, and sample room where salesmen could store their cases, a large hotel lobby, and office in the front. Red velvet carpeting adorned the lobby floors along with brass chandeliers, oak and fir trim and a Steinway grand piano.

Upstairs, a library and parlor were located off the balcony in addition to sixty-three "luxury sleeping rooms." All the rooms were furnished with iron and brass beds and oak furnishings. The original contents were auctioned off in 1976 by the former owners, the Ayres Family, when the building was sold.

It has been a labor of love to restore this grand old hotel to its former glory. Scraps of wallpaper, chips of paint, and old faded stencil designs all helped to direct an authentic restoration of the hotel, which took two-and-a-half years to complete. Particular pains were taken to keep as much of the original detail and recreate others. The upper two stories retain much of the feel of the original rooms, but are larger.

All told, the former sixty-three rooms were reduced to twenty-eight in the restoration. Historic Preservation guidelines require that the original floor plan be retained whenever possible. This has resulted in some rather unique rooms with odd shapes and angles, all of which adds charm to the hotel. The building was built so solid, that in almost one hundred years, the wall had only a three-eighths inch variance from corner to corner. Seth Bullock built it to last, and we're confident that the Bullock will be here another hundred years!

We would like to think Seth would have approved.
Seth Bullock was born in 1849 in the village of Sandwich, Ontario to retired British Major George Bullock and his Scottish wife. Little is known of his boyhood, except that he was frequently at odds with his father's strict attitudes concerning discipline.

Seth arrived in Helena, Montana, in 1867 to become a permanent part of the Western scene. He ran for the Territorial Legislature at the early age of twenty, but was defeated. However, he was successful in being elected as a Republican member of the Territorial Senate of Montana, serving in the 1871 and 1892 sessions, and during which he introduced a resolution memorializing the Congress of the United States to set aside Yellowstone for all time to come as a great national park. The resolution was adopted by the Legislature and shortly thereafter, a bill was introduced in both houses of Congress. Yellowstone Park was established by Federal Statute on March 1, 1872.

In 1873, Bullock was elected Sheriff of Montana territory in Lewis and Clark County. In addition to his other activities, he soon made a mark for himself as an auctioneer and commission merchant in early-day Helena. He entered into a partnership with Sol Star in the hardware business as well as serving as Chief Engineer of the Helena Fire Department.

In 1876, Star and Bullock followed the gold rush to Deadwood, South Dakota to open a soon-successful hardware business in the hell-roaring camp, after sending his bride Martha with their first-born infant daughter back to the security of her Michigan home. Bullock was elected treasurer of the Board of Health and Street Commissioners, organized to combat a threatened smallpox epidemic and which quickly became the first unofficial governmental unit in Deadwood.

The death of Wild Bill Hickok in August of 1876 triggered a growing demand for law and order in Deadwood, resulting in Bullock's appointment as the first Sheriff of Deadwood a few months thereafter.

He quickly appointed several able, fearless deputies and before long order had settled upon Deadwood with little fanfare or gun smoke. With the elimination of the "roughs" from Deadwood, Seth devoted his time to ranching and raising Thoroughbred horses on the ranch he and his partner established at the confluence of the Belle Fourche River and Redwater Creek. He also dabbled in mining, politics, and promotion while continuing to serve as Deputy United States Marshal.

In the spring of 1881, Bullock planted alfalfa on his ranch, which is generally credited as being the introduction of this important crop to the state of South Dakota. Continuing his youthful dedication to conservation, Bullock successfully secured a federal fish hatchery for the Black Hills area, located near modern-day Spearfish.

Bullock became the founder of the town of Belle Fourche (later to become the largest livestock shipping point in the United States and the county seat of Butte County) by persuading the railroad to build through the old site of the DeMore Stage Stop on the Bullock/ Star Ranch and offering free lots for any building moved from the town of Minnesela to his "new" town.

During the Spanish-American War, Bullock volunteered for active service in the Cavalry and was named a Captain of Troop A in Grigsby's Cowboy Regiment. The outfit never saw combat, but did sustain quite a few casualties from typhoid which was rampant in the Louisiana training camp, where they impatiently sat out the short war.

During the 1890s, Bullock continued to maintain a close contact with Teddy Roosevelt. This close personal friendship between the Bullock and Roosevelt families had begun years prior when the two men shared coffee and beans over the tailgate of a chuck wagon on the rangelands near Belle Fourche. Roosevelt, the newly elected Vice President under President McKinley, appointed Bullock as the first Forest Supervisor of the Black Hills Reserve.

In 1905, President Teddy Roosevelt appointed Seth Bullock as United States Marshal for South Dakota. Seth was reappointed in 1909 by President Taft and continued in office for one year under President Woodrow Wilson.

Roosevelt's death in January 1919 was a fearful blow to Captain Bullock who was in a weak, emaciated condition himself. By mid-February, however Bullock was busily engaged in his last act of devotion to his beloved friend. Enlisting the aid of Society of Black Hills Pioneers, he erected a monument to Roosevelt on Sheep Mountain. The peak was renamed Mt. Roosevelt and on its crest Bullock and his fellow pioneers erected a tower constructed of native Black Hills stone. This, the first memorial to Theodore Roosevelt in the United States, was dedicated July 4, 1919.

Trail's end came for Captain Seth Bullock two months later in September 1919 at the age of seventy. His gravesite overlooks the monument he lovingly dedicated to Teddy Roosevelt. His headstone is adorned with many coins and cigars left out of affection for Deadwood's most influential man.

All of the rooms in the Historic Bullock Hotel are unique. With so many different layouts, it feels as though you are in a different hotel each time you stay at the Bullock. From the Roosevelt Suite named after Seth's best friend Teddy Roosevelt, to the most haunted room 313, your experience at the Bullock Hotel will be as unique as the pioneer who built it.

Bullock Hotel Ghostly Encounters

Strong feelings of presence felt inside rooms and in hallway areas of the second and third floor, and the same feeling in Bully's Bar.

Rooms 205, 207, 209, 211, 302, 305, and 314 have all had some sort of paranormal activity reported in them.

Apparition of Seth Bullock helped a lost child in the hotel back to his room.

Items are often moved from one place to another by unseen forces.

Many guests and staff members have reported hearing their name being called by a male voice, when no one is visibly present. Also whistling has been heard in several rooms.

Lights and major appliances turn on and off seemingly by themselves.

An apparition identified as Seth Bullock, has been seen by guests and staff in various areas of the hotel. The most complete apparition of Seth was near the restaurant in 1989.

There have been reports of people being tapped on the shoulder by unseen hands.

Sounds of footsteps are heard throughout the hotel by staff and guests.

Some photographs, taken by guests, have produced anomalies. One particular photo, taken in room 211 shows a white, cloudy figure hovering above the bed.

Plates and glasses shake and take flight of their own accord in the restaurant area.

The apparition of a young girl has been seen in the hotel as well, especially in the basement where children were kept during the typhoid fever and small pox outbreak in Deadwood.

Staff members witnessed movement of several barstools while in Seth's Cellar and upstairs in Bully's Bar.

Paranormal activity seems to increase whenever a staff member whistles, hums, or stands idle.

Cleaning carts have moved on their own accord.

Shower turned on in room 208 by itself and sprayed staff member.

An antique clock that no longer functions in room 305 (Seth's Suite) will chime at times when staff member enter to clean the room.

Toilet paper unrolled to floor by itself right after staff had replaced a new full roll.

Unseen hands have turned off water.

Shadows witnessed by various people on walls or out of the corner of their eye.

During a slow night at the front desk, the mirror on the wall was shaking during a phone call, and then fell to the ground to shatter ONLY the frame around the delicate mirror.

Strong rose and lilac smelling perfume on casino floor when nobody is there; notably in the winter months.

Glasses on floating bar rack in Bully's Bar will knock together.

Chairs next to fireplace in Bully's Bar will re-arrange themselves.

Unplugged radios will turn on by themselves...to a country station. OR the stations will change from a modern channel to a country station on their own.

Piano in Seth's Cellar has played a ragtime tune all by itself.

A strong cigar smoke smell will linger in places that no one has been; let alone smoked a cigar!

A pregnant woman perished during typhoid fever in early days, several guests have heard a woman weeping and a baby crying but when they go to look in hallway, no one is there and the crying had stopped.

A cowboy, during the Day's of '76, was trying to take an afternoon nap when someone kept knocking at his door. He saw a cowboy outside his door and when he opened it, he was not only alone but he was shoved out and his suite door slammed behind him!

CHAPTER 13
Chickamauga Battlefield

3370 LaFayette Road
Fort Oglethorpe, Georgia

Note from author:

I live less than ten minutes from the Chickamauga Battlefield. When I was much younger, I worked at a riding academy and took people for horseback rides through the battlefield. I have heard all of the stories, and even seen a couple of strange happenings that I will relate in this chapter.

The Battle of Chickamauga was second, only to Gettysburg, as the bloodiest battle of the Civil War. Virtually every battlefield is said to be haunted, but Chickamauga seems to be even more haunted than most. There are so many ghosts wandering the grounds, that it would be impossible to reference them all.

The Chickamauga National Battlefield was established in 1890; the park is located just north of the City of Chickamauga, Georgia, and is part of the Chickamauga-Chattanooga National Military Park.

Battle of Chickamauga

The Battle of Chickamauga, named after a creek that runs nearby, was fought on September 19 and 20 of 1863. The two armies battled for two days, but in the end, the Confederate army conquered the Union Soldiers.

During the battle, many soldiers were cared for in the local homes. More than 150,000 troops met on the battlefield and over 35,000 soldiers were killed, wounded, or missing.

After the battle, the bodies of many Union soldiers were left lying in the field; most were later buried in unmarked graves.

Many of the corpses of the Union soldiers lay where they fell in battle for more than two months before they were buried...and they were buried everywhere in the park.

There are no stones to mark these graves and it is said that even today, a park maintenance crew will occasionally uncover bodies where none were previously thought to be located.

The Ghosts

If ghosts do exist, then looking into Civil War ghosts would be a good place to start. The reason for this is that it was one of the bloodiest wars in U.S. history as well as the most gut wrenching as people were forced to fight friends and family at times.

There are many stories that have been told over the years. When I was younger, we would load up a car with our friends and take off to the park to see what we could see. Most times, we would just end up scaring each other. Some of the following stories may be true, some not...that's for you to decide!

Old Green Eyes

Despite all of the tales and stories of strange activity, there is one legend of Chickamauga that remains the most famous of all, "Old Green Eyes." This mysterious entity was given this colorful nickname by park visitors and rangers who have encountered him over the years. Who is he? Well, that's a good question, because there happens to be two very different legends to explain his presence in the park.

The first story (which frankly doesn't seem to match the creature's appearance or behavior) claims that "Old Green Eyes" was a Confederate soldier who had his head blown off during the battle. When he was buried, all that could be found of him was his head as his body had been destroyed. The stories say that his spirit now roams the battlefield at night, moaning and searching for his missing body.

The other legend of "Old Green Eyes" is apparently a much older one...and much more disturbing too. In this case, trustworthy witnesses have reported the creature to be, not a slain soldier, but a creature, which barely even resembles a person. The story states that "Old Green Eyes" was present at Chickamauga long before the Civil War. Some reports claim that the monster was seen moving among the dead at a place called Snodgrass Hill, after the battle was over.

Note by author:

I have been to Snodgrass Hill on horseback many times and it IS very spooky!!! Even the horses got "spooked!"

Some people claim to feel that they are being watched as they are in the park. Over the years, thousands have claimed to have seen Green Eyes. The first sighting may have been at the battle itself, or even earlier.

According to various sources, other tales claim Green Eyes existed before the Civil War and circulated among the soldiers during the fighting, or that the spirit existed as early as the Native American occupation of the land where the battlefield is now located.

Visitors and staff members claim to have seen green, glowing eyes coming toward them in the darkness and have heard the sounds of a soldier moaning in despair. In the early 1970s, two different and unrelated people had accidents near the same place in the park, wrecking their cars after reportedly seeing these glowing eyes!

In 1980, a Fort Oglethorpe resident said she encountered a ghostly being with green eyes on a cold, foggy night in the park. She had just gotten off work and was taking a shortcut through the park on her way home. She nudged her car slowly through the fog-enshrouded park, about a half-mile from Wilder Tower. It was raining and foggy, so she was going very slowly. She was going through the S-curve past Wilder Tower, when she saw something big in the road about eye level, and all she could see were these big green eyes.

It was so foggy that she couldn't see a body...she got closer and it just disappeared.

The woman said that she always thought the tale of the ghostly green-eyed beast was a myth and never would have "believed it in a million years," but now she says she won't step foot in the park after nightfall!

Note by author:
I had an experience at the same Wilder Tower that was mentioned in the above account.

One late afternoon, while my girlfriend and I were out riding our horses, we stopped at the tower for a rest. We decided to climb the (seemed like thousands of steps) to the top of the tower. There was a big metal door that you went though and then up that long winding staircase. The only light you could see was through tiny windows every so often.

We finally reached the top, out of breath and our legs weak. We looked down and it was a beautiful sight! The cannons still stood as monuments over the huge field, as the sun started to set. We both knew that we should not have been in the park at night because of all of the strange stories we had heard since childhood, but we sat down a few minutes before our long trek back down.

All of the sudden, we heard a big CLANG and the horses were going crazy! We rushed to the front and looked down to where we entered the tower. NOTHING.

The horses settled down, so we calmed down a little. The sun had gone down by then, so we carefully picked our way back down the stairs. When we got to the bottom and tried to open the door. It wouldn't budge! Well, just image two teenaged girls standing in the pitch dark inside what we had heard was a "haunted" tower!

We screamed to the top of our lungs for about fifteen minutes, when a park ranger pulled up in his car. We were in tears by then as we asked him why he locked us in.

"I didn't lock you in, that's what I was coming to do...lock the door," he said as he tried to open the door. The door was locked from the OUTSIDE with a padlock.

He pulled out his keys and opened the door for us. We both rushed out and were shaking so hard that we couldn't stand up.

"I am the only park ranger on duty tonight, so NOBODY else locked the door. You girls should know better than to be in the park after dark. I have seen lots of unexplained things happen," the park ranger told us.

He told us that he would follow us to a main road with houses along the way so that we could get back to the barn. We jumped on our horses and took off as if a bat out of Hell was following us! HE DIDN'T HAVE TO TELL US TWICE!

I was a trail guide and took people for rides through the battlefield, but NEVER, EVER was I caught in the park after dark again!

Green Eyes, in its various forms, is not the only phantom people claim to see in the park. There is also a ghost believed to haunt Snodgrass Hill, which saw some of the fiercest fighting and is home to the Snodgrass family cabin, which served as a field hospital to both Union and Confederate soldiers during the battle.

Note from author:

Again, this happened to me on more than one occasion. My group of friends sometimes gathered at Wiser Tower. We were out there a little late one night, and starting scaring each other with "ghost" stories. All of the sudden, we all saw a light way down the old railroad tracks that ran by the tower. Of course, we had all heard the story about the soldier with the lantern...but we clearly saw it. Stupidly, we started walking down the railroad tracks, but the light seemed to get farther and farther away from us. It never wavered, and we never caught up to it!

After darkness fell on the last day of the battle, within hours of the last shots being fired, women were seen searching the battlefield by lantern light. It has been reported that these eerie lights, along with the voices and cries of the women, are still present on the field today.

The Lady in White

Aside from Old Green Eyes, there is more weirdness on the grounds. Gunshots are sometimes heard in the distance, and marching is heard. A soldier is supposed to walk the roads at night. If he sees you, he is said to stare at you until you leave.

One famous ghost that has been sighted by many people on many different occasions over the years since the war is the lady in white. It is said that this lady was the bride-to-be, whose fiancée was killed in the battle. According to this story, she still walks the area in a wedding dress, searching for him. Even after all of these years, she has supposedly never found him.

It is believed that many of the dead soldiers were buried in the battlefield, but the exact locations are unknown. Several times people have encountered soldiers that disappeared into thin air in a flash.

On the evening of September 20, 1863, darkness settled across the battered land near the Tennessee River. The battle of Chickamauga had just ended. Women crept onto the field, their lanterns bobbing in the murky shadows.

As they discovered the bodies of their loved ones on this southeastern Tennessee battlefield, they let out cries of sorrow. Many years later, these sounds and lights remind us that these women are still lingering in the battlefield, looking for their loved ones.

Visitors to the park seem to be fine in the daytime; it is at night when the creepy things happen.

There are said to be many ghosts and spirits wandering the woods and fields of Chickamauga. Rangers and visitors report many unusual noises on the grounds, including sounds of men moaning and crying; shouts and screams when no one is present; and the sounds of horses galloping…where no horses ever appear.

Some visitors, and even crewmembers, tell of feeling as though they are being watched in the woods at night. **(Who would want to be there at night???)**

Others report seeing the bushes move mysteriously, as though a squad of invisible soldiers were passing by. One of the rangers was even told by a "well-known minister" that he had witnessed a man on horseback ride past him at Chickamauga.... although the rider had no head.

If you ever visit Chickamauga, keep an eye out for Old Green Eyes. You don't want to wander too close to him!

CHAPTER 14
The Carleton House Bed & Breakfast

803 N. Main
Bonham, Texas 75418
800-382-8033
www.carletonhouse.com

Located in the heart of historic downtown Bonham, Texas, just one hour northeast of Dallas, is the Historic Carleton House Bed & Breakfast. The House was built in 1888 by A.J. Clendenen, who operated a grocery and produce store on the square. In 1914, Dr. J. C. Carleton purchased the home for his family and electricity was introduced at this time.

This newly renovated three story Victorian, listed on the National Register of Historic Homes. features a large entrance hall, a parlor, dining room with ceiling mural, music room, breakfast area, and a large staircase leading to the bedrooms. We are also fortunate enough to have one of the two remaining carriage stones left in Fannin County.

THE ROOMS

All rooms are located on the second floor. They include a TV, VCR, old movies, lamps, alarm clock, central heat and air, reading and writing materials, games, and playing cards.

Each of the rooms has a private bathroom equipped with a claw foot tub or relaxing bubble baths or quick showers if you are in a hurry. Also included is an assortment of bath items stocked for guests' pleasure.

Personal experiences of the owner, Karen Halbrook:

We are the owners of an 1888 Victorian home on the National Historic Register. We've been operating as a Bed & Breakfast for the past ten years and have heard several stories from our guests as well as our own experiences.

My mother still insists that a ghost threw her makeup bag off of a washstand in her room. To this day, she will not stay upstairs in my house alone.

While working on the house on more than one occasion, things would get "lost." Jokingly I would speak to the "ghost" and say, "I'll just have to burn the house down and you'll have no where to live." Things always seemed to turn up shortly thereafter. So not really believing in ghosts (or not wanting to see any), this went on through the construction phase of the house.

After opening for business, I woke up about 4:30 a.m. one morning to the distinct smell of bacon frying. We had guests at the time, but surely, none of them would be cooking in the kitchen. So I got up and went into the hallway, fully awake, and could still smell the bacon.

I went downstairs to the kitchen to find no one there. **(I guess ghosts get hungry too).**

Another instance was waking up to the smell of an old-timie perfume odor that filled the bedroom. I awoke my husband and he, too, could smell the perfume. There were no guests in the house that night so it couldn't have been from anyone but a ghost.

Another night (I'm not sure if you want to hear this one) I woke up to what smelled like a baby's "wet" diaper. I got up to investigate but didn't smell this anywhere else but in our room.

One evening my friend and I were playing with the Ouija board…just for fun. This turned up some interesting facts. After a period of nonsense and laughing, we settled down and tried asking the board if someone died in the house. In the spirit of fun, we closed our eyes. The message indictor flew over to "yes." When asked "when," the answer "68" was given to us. When asked "who died here" it gave us the initials "too." Each thinking the other was pushing it; we sneaked peeks only to find neither of us was actually touching the indicator. We were trying to keep up with it. My friend was crying by this time and I was covered with goose bumps. To this day, the mysterious "too" is still unknown.

Since we have finished the restoration and been open for ten years, various small items end up missing. A day or two will pass and then I will open a drawer to find the item on top and centered in the drawer where I had previously searched. I jokingly tease that it must have been put there by the ghost!

As far as all the incidences, none are threatening; all have been childlike pranks.

Imagine my surprise when I received the photo of the image on the stairway during the estate sale of one of the previous occupants of the house. That photo was taken between 1914 and the 1920s when the Carleton family still lived in the house.

It appears to be an image of a small girl holding onto the stair rail and walking down the stairs!

We have not advertised this to our guests in the past because they seemed frightened by the possibility of the presence of ghosts. Guests, of their own experience, have questioned us the following day of the possibility of a ghost. We've heard that some people are more sensitive to the ghosts than others and that if you believe, they will appear to you.

While working on the house, several other incidences occurred in the form of smells such as old perfume and bacon wafting through the house in the middle of the night. Objects turning up missing then later being found placed gingerly in sight, and beds shaking in the middle of the night for no apparent reason.

Over the years, guests have reported seeing a child in the window from outside (when there were no children in the house), door knobs jiggling, tapping on windows, footsteps and closet doors opening during the night as well as items being knocked off of tables, and armoire doors opening and closing while the guest was watching TV.

P.S. *Just an example: as soon as we started to respond to you after looking at your website, the computer started acting up. I guess Molly doesn't want the word to get out!*

Our newest location, The Carleton Casual House, has been fully restored to accommodate guests wanting ground floor rooms or those traveling with young children. It is perfect for families or large groups yet can accommodate couples.

The Carleton Casual House

CHAPTER 15
The Dock Street Theatre

135 Church Street
Charleston, South Carolina 29401
Phone: 843-720-3968 Fax: 843-720-3847 Email:
ParhamC@ci.charleston.sc.us

Thank you to Christopher G. Parham, Theatre Manager

*Known as one of the most haunted places in Charleston, it is home
to the spirit of a prostitute as well as the father of John Wilkes Booth.*

The History

The Dock Street Theatre, located in the heart of Charleston's
Historic District at 135 Church Street, is within easy walking
distance of many downtown accommodations. It was the first
building in America to be designed solely for theatrical performances.

The original Dock Street Theatre was built on this site in 1735
and was the first true theatre in the colonies. It stood roughly where
the stage is today and ran east to west, as opposed to north to south
like it is today. The structure was reported to have been destroyed by
fire.

In 1809, the present day structure was created to be the Planters Hotel. The hotel was remolded in 1835, and according to period photographs, has not changed at all in exterior photographs since at least 1875. During that time, the Planters Hotel was one of the largest and most luxurious in Charleston.

After the War Between the States, the building fell into neglect and was badly damaged by the great earthquake of 1886. The building was soon after abandoned and became a haunted relic of times past.

In the mid 1930s, the Works Progress Administration restored the hotel structure to its original appearance and converted the interior into a theatre once again.

The new structure was modeled after a composite of London's 18th century theaters, designed with a "pit" for the common people, a "gallery" for women, and "boxes" at the balcony level for the city's elite citizens as well as having modern technical equipment installed.

A local architect filled the theater with beautiful woodwork carved from native Cypress trees, or salvaged architectural items from Charleston's antebellum mansions.

What is now the stage was a four-story block of hotel rooms. What is now the house was a courtyard, some of which may still be seen while passing through the gallery.

A Rockefeller grant installed Dubose Heyward as resident writer. Heyward and his wife Dorothy were famous for writing the play "Porgy and Bess," which George and Ira Gerswin used as the basis of their American opera.

The theater's programming included artists, such as dancers Ruth St. Denis and Martha Graham. Until the 1970s, Emmett Edward Robinson was the theater's managing director who handled programming as well as the Footlight Players productions.

In 1978, Julian Wiles, who had worked closely with Robinson, founded the Charleston Stage Company, which is now one of the state's largest arts organizations. The company presents 120 performances at the Dock Street Theatre each season.

The theater is owned and now managed by the City of Charleston.

It houses arts organizations on its third floor and the city's office of cultural affairs, as well as producing both the annual Piccolo and Moja festivals, which have some performances at the theater. The annual Spoleto Festival USA also holds concerts and performances at the theater.

Each year, more than 600 events are performed at the Dock Street Theatre for about 100,000 theater patrons.

Infamous Guest

One of the hotels most infamous guests was Junius Brutus Booth, actor and father of President Lincoln's assassin. Booth would stay at the hotel while performing in the city.

According to a newspaper account, Booth was scheduled to appear at the Charleston Theatre on March 13, 1838. After leaving the theatre on March 12 in the company of a Mr. Flynn (his manager) they returned to their lodgings at the Planters Hotel. Both gentlemen were occupying the same room.

Between one and two o'clock in the morning Mr. Flynn was awakened by receiving a tremendous blow over the right eye. He sprang up in bed, and discovered Mr. Booth in the act of aiming another blow at him with one of the cast iron firedogs taken from the fireplace in the room.

Mr. Flynn made an effort to avoid the second blow, that he knew was coming, but received it over the left eye with such force that it broke the firedog. He leapt from bed and escaped the room with Mr. Booth in close pursuit; trying to inflict other wounds.

They finally wrestled and fell. Mr. Booth, while laboring under the exhilaration of madness, had the advantage of phenomenal strength!

The calls of Mr. Flynn finally brought assistance and Mr. Booth was placed under restraint. He was kept that way until he recovered from his malfunction of mind.

On March 20, he appeared at the Charleston Theatre as Richard III.

The Ghost Tales
Some say they can still hear the screams of Mr. Flynn up and down the backstage halls (where the hotel rooms were once located), trying to escape the attack.

Actors and stagehands, as well, have claimed to see a man in a top hat and black cloak looming in the balcony boxes during rehearsals; perhaps an actor from days gone by is watching them.

Another story related to the building's history is the story of Nettie Dickerson, who was believed to be a lady of ill fame who frequented the hotel with her wealthy planter gentlemen clients. It is believed that her life ended when the wrought iron balcony on the front of the building was struck by lightning while she was standing on it. Her spirit never left the building. Whenever there is an event in the theatre, she can be seen walking the upper corridors of the building that lead to the old hotel ballroom (now a reception area.)

The unusual thing is that when they remolded the hotel to make way for the theatre, they poured over a foot of concrete over the old floor to create a new floor. Apparently, Nettie still walks on the original level because she cannot be seen from the mid-calf down!

CHAPTER 16
The 1891 Castle Inn of New Orleans

1539 4th Street
New Orleans, LA 70130
Fax: 504-895-2231 Reservations: 1-888-826-0540
E-mail: info@creolegardens.com

Note from author:

I wrote about the Castle Inn in a previous book a couple of years ago. Unfortunately, Katrina hit Louisiana and took the Castle out of commission for the time being. This impact is typical for so many businesses affected by Hurricane Katrina.

I emailed owner, Andrew Craig, to see if I might use the stories again in this book. This is when he told me the news. He informed me that they had bought another hotel, The Creole Gardens Bed and Breakfast. The Creole Gardens is also haunted and is fully operational.

In the next chapter, you will hear about this new hotel. I suggested that we put the chapter about The Castle in the book so you can hear some great, spooky stories. Thanks, Andrew, and good luck with your new venture!

Stories told by Andrew Craig, one of the owners of the Castle Inn:

Yes, we do have a real "live" resident ghost. In fact, we think we have at least two.

When we first took over the 1891 Castle Inn in 1998, we had no idea we would be sharing our mansion with spirits—at least the non-flammable kind! When one of our staff repeatedly reported seeing a male apparition standing by the window in Room 11, we did not quite believe it. Then, when guests reported strange occurrences taking place fairly regularly, we began to think that there might be something to it.

Intrigued and bewildered, we went to the previous owners and asked if they had ever encountered anything out of the ordinary. They claimed they had not.

Our guests and employees reported strange and unexplained encounters: Objects moving by themselves, electric lights and appliances turning on and off on their own, unexplained sounds, lots of footsteps, water faucets turning on and off in empty bathrooms, and brief glimpses of a "translucent man" standing in corners and on the front porch late at night.

Cool, huh? This is the kind of stuff that makes you question precepts of reality and mortality. We are now pretty much believers although I am still waiting for the penny to creep up the door by itself. Whoopee!

What we have learned about our spirits is the result of several ghost researchers' "readings" and testimonials of our guests, visitors, and staff. Here is what we think we have—two ghosts—perhaps more. Dates and names seem to be hard to nail down, but based on the "facts," both of our ghosts left this material world at least 100 years ago—or probably even longer!

Our first ghost was a paid servant, a horse carriage driver, who acted as a gentleman's gentleman. He was a very light skinned black man who spoke several languages, loved the ladies, loved music, drank far too much, smoked and was quite the prankster. Sadly, he accidentally killed himself in a smoky fire, set either through smoking in bed or by knocking over a heating pot. He was so drunk he did not wake and suffocated to death. His spirit remains in our mansion because it chooses to.

After all, he always believed that his rightful place was in the main mansion and not in the servant's quarters. He is the one responsible for the coughing and whistling heard in the hallways, objects moving or being hidden (ask about the receipts in the microwave) and is the "translucent man" often seen in mirrors or briefly seen out of the corner of a guest's eyes. He loves to play with radios, televisions, ceiling fans, and lights. If you cannot find an object in your room, look in a drawer or in a place where you would not leave it. (Like the guests who, upon checking out, could not find the receipts of the past four days of shopping and travel which the husband had collected in his wallet). His wife found them all in the microwave after they searched the room from top to bottom.

Our second ghost is a little girl who drowned in a small pond on the former grounds of the local plantation before it was subdivided to make room for a rapidly growing New Orleans. She was wearing a white dress and was barefoot at the time. She wanders the neighborhood in search of her mother and is a frequent visitor to the Castle Inn. She is the one responsible for water turning on and off, women being touched on the leg (as if your kid were trying to wake you up for pancakes on Sunday morning) and little bare feet running up and down hallways.

All of our guests indicated that they were not frightened by their encounters, just perplexed and bemused. Interestingly, our "best" encounters come from guests who did not know we have ghosts or discounted the whole thing as a marketing gimmick. We have had dozens upon dozens of very vivid tales told to us by guests who have nothing to prove or gain by their stories.

Come stay with us. Maybe you will get lucky and have an experience. If you do, tell us or write them down in our guest book. We won't laugh (although your friends and family may think you had too good of a time in ol' N'awlins before you went to bed)!

The Ghost Testimonials

(Taken from the Guest Book at the Castle Inn)

My girlfriend Millie and I stayed the last four nights with you, three of which were in the Napoleon Room 5. I had already written something of this in your guest book. I wanted to describe what happened to me the last two nights of my stay, especially since one thing in particular I didn't read in anyone else's testimony.

We opted to sleep with the lights on that night (like that would really help us). I heard the sounds of someone moving furniture all over the house, like my friend the two nights before had mentioned. I also had a sense of someone watching us in the room, but had not seen anyone. At 1:30 a.m., my friend and I starkly awoke at the exact same moment, feeling an immense presence in the room. It was much larger than the presence of a human. During this feeling, I had the sensation of a soft caress on my foot and up my leg, followed by fingers caressing my scalp and hair. I could not think about sleeping the rest of the night, but continued to have the sensation of someone watching me until about 4:30 a.m. At that point, all noise died out.

The hurricane was starting to move in and we were the only ones in the house that night. Around 10:30 p.m., I heard the "normal" noises of furniture moving. At 11:30 p.m., I heard the distant sound of a small child's music box playing in the hall. It lasted over a minute. As soon as I laid my head down to go to sleep, I had the sensation again of a soft caress on my foot and up my leg as if someone was gently jumping on it. This was quite a strange feeling! When leaving the house at 4:00 a.m. to catch a taxi for an early flight, my friend turned around to look up at the balcony of our room and saw a dark figure in the window watching us leave. Maybe he or she was sad to see us go.

Since I had so many encounters with the little girl, I would be curious to know if I somehow look like her mother. Do you all have any additional information or resources about her and/or her mother?

We heard rapping noises in the bedroom at 1:30 a.m. on the 11th. Television changer moved across the room on the night of the 11th.

We were really looking forward to our stay at the Castle Inn, having found it on the internet in the UK. We spent three nights in the Jazz Emporium Room and two nights in the Gothic Sanctuary Room (10). On the second night Judy, my partner, awoke with a "start" as the bed began moving. Then she felt someone, or something, sit on the bottom of the bed. She woke me up because she first thought it was me turning in the bed. I missed it all. At first, she was afraid and wanted to turn on the light so she could use the bathroom. In the Gothic Sanctuary, our radio kept turning itself off as if someone was using a snooze button. I checked it all out. One night the light came on by itself. The last night, we left the ceiling fan on in the adjoining room only to find that this morning it was turned off. Yes, it's true—something else lives in this house too!

When we arrived, we did not even know that is was "haunted." Did not see any ghosts, but a lot of creaking in the night and someone moved my sheet very deliberately into a strange position on the floor! The maid maybe?

There was no ghostly activity...DARN. Our teenage daughter and two of her friends stayed in the Laveaux attic room and heard noises—"felt" someone was in the room, had something brush against their legs (like a cat that wasn't there) and ENJOYED IT ALL. We got lots of picture orbs!

Ghosts—we had a few. The turning on and off lights in the bathroom, the radio coming on by itself...three times, something moved across the floor...I did not see it but my husband heard it. Last night—felt a cat move across the bed. Something moved the shower curtain by itself. We had a few other encounters—our shade flew up on Monday morning, and the ghost hid my husband's glasses. Fortunately, we found them on the floor at the foot of the bed. Nothing else happened to us directly, but we did hear a lot of movement in the room around us.

The first night of our stay was quiet and relaxing. The second night, I was taking a bath and heard three loud knocks on the bathroom door. Thinking it was my husband, I called "come in," three times. Then I heard the knocks again. This time I yelled louder and finally my husband heard me calling. He said he was not knocking on the door, nor did he hear anything (knocking). Later that evening I heard a cat meow.

Our last evening, we decided to call upon the spirits of the house to speak to us using a Ouija board we had brought with us from New York. Immediately, we were in contact with a "spirit." His name was Henry. He claimed that he was born in 1854. He was a card player and used his great talents for making a living as he had many children for which to provide. He claimed to have only lived to be thirty-nine years old. We asked many questions. He was kind to answer all of them. He stated that he likes Room 8 (part of Room 7 suite) in this house the best. At this time, I have no clue as to which room that is.

Anyway, during this session we began taking digital photos of the room. Immediately, white lights and shapes were showing up in the photos. Most of the lights or spirits were directly over the light. We took many photos of the same spot—the spirits were moving around the room. As they moved over by the door, I snapped another photo over the bed—the lights were gone because now the spirits have shifted to the other side of the room. By the door there was a spirit sitting in the red chair. We caught on camera a vortex, and I mean a large vortex of energy flying up from the chair towards the painting above. It's a really neat photo. Anyhow, we gave Henry our blessings and let him go.

This was a great stay for an amateur "ghost hunter." Yesterday, we left our key in the room and the door locked automatically. (Normally it requires key to lock it). After arguing about it, we went to get an extra set. When I arrived back at the room, the door was wide open and the light was on. This was kind of spooky. Later that night there was a small "ghost hunt" with amazing results. It was humming outside our door. The dog (they allow pets) also heard it and kept staring at the door. Earlier he went to the door and started gnawing (scratching sounds outside the door).

I went to sleep with a necklace on, and awoke to find it on the table next to the couch, on top of my camera. When I awoke the next morning, both my shoes and my brother's were arranged in a pattern on the floor.

My friend and I woke up this morning to find our stuff had been moved around. She had her suitcase on a couch and it was open. My suitcase was on the floor and it was closed. This morning we found our suitcases had switched places. Hers was not closed and mine was open. I had thrown my shoes randomly on the floor, and this morning they were very neatly laid at the foot of my bed.

In addition, we both had some of our stuff on a table in the room and we are not sure if the table was turned around or if our stuff was moved. Nothing was hidden, but it was all moved around.

On our first night, we kept hearing footsteps up and down stairs. Tina kept feeling something trying to pass through her. I woke up about 2:00 a.m. and saw a mist-like shape at the end of the bed and in front of the dresser. Also, we kept smelling flowers and tobacco smoke earlier in the evening (the castle is a non-smoking inn).

On our second day, we kept smelling flowers and tobacco smoke. We were gone all day in the French Quarter. We came back around 2:00 p.m and took a nap. After we awoke, we were getting cleaned up and Tina was making the bed when she found some ashes in our room. We took them down and showed them to Nicholas (our general manager).

We then went out again for a walk. When we returned, Tina checked the bed and found some more of the little chunks of ashes. Upon going to bed, nothing happened until 11:00 p.m. or so. Tina then started saying that it was passing through her again. The bed shook a few times after that and I awoke and could not fall back to sleep. Then I noticed that there was this black shadow moving about the room. I finally fell back to sleep and slept pretty good after that.

For quite a long time on the first night, I saw a large shadow moving around the room. The bed was pushed once and my girlfriend and I heard footsteps continuously, up and down the stairs outside of the room until about 6:00 a.m.

On our second night, we think the spirits in the house were used to us. The window rattled twice without the help of wind or traffic and we saw a flash of light in the room. It was like a camera flash…very strange.

Our bed shook and when we returned from an outing, we found a washcloth wedged in between the windowsill in the bathroom. It was not like that when we left. SPOOKY!

We did not "see" any ghosts, but we did have a few strange things happen. Our radio frequently turned itself on and off. We kept checking to see if the radio alarm was set, but it was not. I felt something thump from the underside of the bed twice. We left the bathroom light on as a nightlight, but by 1:30 a.m. when I woke up, it was off. This morning, the bed shook twice! I also felt the sensation of a cat jumping on the bed, taking a few steps and lying down next to me.

I was curious. Is there really a ghost in the Voodoo room? We heard some footsteps that sounded like a child running but there are not any children in here, so we think it was the little girl that drowned.

We heard armor clang first, then heard snoring and footsteps in room 10 during our second night of stay.

Someone has been watching me all day!

Our TV kept turning on at night after we turned out the lights.

I heard footsteps on the stairway although I knew there was no one there. Went to the third floor to see. As I started coming down the stairs, I heard a man cough on the landing. However, I knew the house was empty at the time. Was it the ghost?

The light flashed on by itself and the fan turned on after the flash of light.

It's all a sham, what a big hoax. You can explain it all with air pressure, air currents, creaky stairs, and a ghost. "He" dimmed the lights half an inch to the left. He turned on the faucet and put the toilet to the test. I closed the door to room 5, he opened it again much to my surprise. The radio clicked and played music from 1955.
On the last night of our stay, there was an "occupant" occupying but they were not breathing. I am sure he had a favorite bed with the best set of linens. A chilled breeze moved though the hall, disturbing the curtains. Therefore, I asked that "something" a question, "If you were me, would you want to see? I'm counting to three." The ghost showed ME; the door began to creak. So I quickly scurried back to my room, locked the door, knowing all the while that this action could not protect me. Through the peephole I peered, I unlocked the door when I felt no danger near. I heard door 7 still squeak and I said, "I know that you're here, just as you are aware of me. But I will thank you if you would not bother me tonight." And with that, I turned in. My last thought of the night was…I don't believe such things that others fear most. As for rooms 5, 6 and 7…they harbor a ghost!

The ceiling fan began turning and the pull string was missing from it. Also, my husband said he saw me in the mirror up the first step of steps; however, I was all the way at the top of the staircase.

The ghosts kept us up two nights in a row. The first day our TV kept coming unplugged. We would leave and upon returning, it would be unplugged again; this happened three times.

The second night was amazing and frightening at the same time. We saw this little girl by the stairways. My wife saw the black male ghost once or twice that night. Therefore, we finally got to sleep around 5:00 a.m. We also heard steps running up and down our stairs. No one else was staying on our side of the mansion that night. Around 3:00 a.m., the last thing we heard was a little girl giggling. We had brought some food back from quite a large dinner when Aly and I decided to reheat it. That was when we found our gift cards from Jeijer in the microwave! Now, I assure you, being the type of person I am, I always know where things are. They were in my wallet no more than an hour before. Then they ended up in our microwave.

Is this house haunted? I would say yes, unless of course I was drinking that night—which I wasn't!

Our shower turned on by itself at 1:30 a.m.

Still wondering who moved our bed so far away from the wall late one night while we were out.

Our bed shook three times!

I had just lain down for bed. I started to hear a voice talking. It lasted about 2-3 seconds. I could not understand what was said, but it sounded like a scratched record or one being played backwards.

I awoke from my sleep to a chill, and a light that came from one side of my room to the other; hovering over my head in the bed. This was just before dawn...then it passed through the walls.

Before we went to bed, we noticed all the lampshades in our room were twisted and lopsided. I made them level and went to sleep. When we woke up, they were all back to the same positions as before.

I heard something like footsteps and keys rattling in the hallway, so I turned on the lights and looked out. There was no one there. I went back to bed when the overhead ceiling fan started turning and then I heard the water in the bathtub turn on. Then I heard keys rattling. I went to turn the water off, and went back to bed. The footsteps continued in the outside hall.

Felt something stroking my face.

We had an early night—we were in bed reading with one of the side lamps on. I turned it off around 10:30–10:45 p.m. My husband and I chatted for a bit and then, all of the sudden, the overhead light came on. The only switch being across the room. I joked that it must have been the ghost. My husband got back up to turn it off.

In the morning, we checked to see if the light could be turned on any other way, but it could not have been. About 2:00 a.m., I felt someone touch my leg and I felt cold. Then I heard my husband say, "Look, there's lights on the ceiling," and I looked up and saw them. I tried to scream, but it came out silent as in a dream where you try to yell, but it would not come out. I felt chills and sweated for nearly three hours. I felt like someone was watching me.

Woke up in the middle of the night and saw a light on the ceiling. Also, someone was shaking my husband's side of the bed.

The first night, we were in room 12 and I had a dream that there was a man sitting on the couch in our room. He had caramel colored skin, black hair and dark eyes. I think he was wearing something tan colored. He was cute! I talked to Wynette about it and she said that sounded like the description of the ghost so maybe I wasn't dreaming!

The next night I was awakened by a man's voice in my ear. He was talking in a different language—French, Spanish—I'm not sure. I was half-asleep and he scared me. The following two nights, there was a TV up really loud in Room 11 next door. Carried informed me that no one had been staying in Room 11 those two nights! (Spoooooooky!) Then finally, I woke up to someone singing in our room. My friend, Kim heard it too.

After that, we asked him to leave us alone and he did. Neither one of us had been getting enough sleep because of him. After I woke up from my initial dream, I knew his name and forgot it. It was R-O something. I think like Rode or something like that. Anyway, even though he spooked us, he didn't do anything harmful or make me feel unsafe.

Last night I got scared. Up late and noises all over the place. Doors slamming from about 2:30 a.m. until 5:00 a.m. I played the tough guy, but was pretty freaked out.

I went to the bathroom. When I came back into the bedroom, my glass had been moved across the room.

Got a lot of pictures with orbs.

Chapter 17
The Creole Gardens Guesthouse Bed & Breakfast

1415 Prytania St.
New Orleans, LA 70130
Toll Free: 1-866-569-8700
info@creolegardens.com

Hey, Sugar. We invite you to come and stay with us at the Creole Gardens Guesthouse Bed and Breakfast, located in the New Orleans Lower Garden District, one block away from the famed St. Charles Avenue Streetcar line.

This unique New Orleans B & B is located only minutes away from many famous places. The French Quarter, Magazine Street, the Central Business District, Morial Convention Center, Tulane and Loyola Universities, Canal Street, Algiers Ferry, and the Riverwalk stores are only a few.

You think that's a mouthful? Well, Lafayette Cemetery, the D-Day Museum, Audubon Zoo, The Aquarium of the Americas, and The Louisiana Superdome are also close neighbors.

Just up the road are Commander's Palance, Upperline, Emeril

Lagasse's Delmonico, Cannon's, Pascal Manale's, Copeland's, Fat Harry's Pub, and Slice Pizza.

All the more important, Mardi Gras parades pass one block away on St. Charles Avenue!

WHEW!!! What don't they have??

The Creole Gardens Guesthouse B & B comprises two 1849 historic mansions and a two story servants' quarters centered on a banana courtyard and fountain—hugely popular with New Orleans wedding planners.

The property was renovated in 2004 and meets the latest hotel fire, safety and building codes while maintaining the charm of a historic antebellum mansion with "dependency" quarters. Each of our 26 individually decorated rooms offer air conditioning, television, free high speed internet, 10/100 ports and of course, private baths.

Our **Manse,** or Main mansion, houses our office, dining room & kitchen, sitting room, four guest rooms, including a huge private honeymoon apartment with private balcony overlooking the New Orleans skyline. Three of the Manse guest rooms have stunning broad heart-pine flooring and endless original historic detail—each with huge bathrooms with both showers as well as clawfoot tubs.

Wake up and head down to a complimentary, full southern breakfast in our dining room or take a plate outside and to enjoy our banana courtyard.

The Ghosts

Yes, the Creole Gardens Guesthouse Bed and Breakfast is haunted. We know of at least seven people who have died on the premises over the past 150 years.

More to come as we compile stories from our construction workers, employees, former employees under the previous ownership, etc.

Below are *excerpts* of emails sent to me by owner, Andrew Craig:

***

Yes, I was unsure about the male. I didn't think that he was attached to the house. I'm fairly certain that he followed us back in from somewhere in the city, it happens quite often. Sometimes certain spirits, particularly the nasty ones, realize when people are sensitive to them and try to make contact. It's not a particularly fun thing to have happen.

The slave woman seemed to be a very peaceful spirit; she was a very calming presence. That is an unbelievable story. Funny enough, you're one of about 20 people who have seen that slave woman.

Thanks for the orb picture, by the way. I found it to be quite interesting. It looks as if the two properties have very strong manifestations in them.

As for the angry man, I don't think I have ever heard of him before. It's just fascinating to me that people actually see these things because I've never seen or felt anything at the Creole or at the castle, which is supposedly the 7th most haunted place in the United States. I am going to pass your chilling account on to the owners, who love to receive confirmation that we have "spirit," if you will. We were afraid that Katrina blew them all away, but we're still hearing stories. And YOU! just start thinking about when you're coming back, young woman! I'll let you hang out at the castle for an evening and see if you pick up on one of the four known entities at that property. It would be interesting to see what you come back with.

***

February 28, 2006
Greetings from Germany
I was most interested to see that you put up a link for the ghosts in your Guesthouse on your site, since you didn't have the link up when I stayed with you. It didn't even occur to me to tell you about the lady that I saw, when I stayed with you, because quite frankly I've seen ghosts since I was a little girl. So it's not an uncommon experience for me.

My husband and I stayed with you on the 11th and 12th of October 2003, in the Miss Gipsy Shafer's Sapho lounge room. At around 12:45 a.m. on the twelfth I woke up. When I looked over at my husband, I realized that there was a lady perched on his side of the bed. She was a black lady and had on a whitish colored head kerchief and a dress, much like a servant in the early 1800s would wear. She was making a stroking motion with her hand like she was stroking the side of his face, and looking down at him with a look of utter love and adoration. The scene itself was very maternal, like a mother stroking a sleeping child. He never awoke, but I think on some level he may have known that she was there, because he had a smile on his face in his sleep, and when he awoke the next morning, he said that it was the best he had slept for months. I watched her for a couple minutes and she never looked up at me, so I just kind of laughed to myself and went back to sleep.

So I would be interested to know the history of your house and if anyone else has seen her. I'm also curious to know if there is some sort of malevolent male presence there as well. The second night I woke up because I heard crying coming from the bathroom area, and there was the shadowy figure of a male by the door. He was a very angry male, so I quickly told him to get out. When he left, the crying stopped and everything was peaceful again. I'm not sure if he was already in the house, or if he was something that just followed us in from the city, sometimes I have a sort of nasty habit of attracting these things.

***

December 26, 2003 1:40 PM
Ghosts at Creole Gardens

My friend Diann & I stayed in Rooms 6 & 7 during the summer. My sister Wanda visited us there and all three of us spent lots of time on the front porch and in the courtyard. Had a wonderful time, and we really enjoyed ourselves.

I even had "someone, or something" try to get into bed with me just before daybreak. I felt the mattress sag as if someone—or something—was kneeling on the bed and leaning over me. I was afraid to look so I just told it to go away, and it did. Now I wish I had looked!

I have been meaning to send this picture to you for months. In the courtyard behind the mansion is a lattice panel with a chair on the other side, the "face" appears to be sitting in the chair just above the lattice. This is in the top left corner of the courtyard picture. I wish now that I had brought the digital camera with me so the picture would be of a better quality.

If you have an explanation as to what the "face" might be—or whom— I would love to hear it.

Loved seeing Andy and Miss Karen on the Travel Channel's Halloween Haunted Hotels!

Hope to return soon!

***

Thanks, Andy…we are still trying to plan on coming down next summer. I just fell in love with New Orleans when we were there. I do not know if I told you what we experienced when we were there. We were in room 7, and Joselyn was in the bathroom curling her hair when my conditioner flew at her, hitting the garbage can. Traci was taking a shower, reached for her shampoo and it was not there. She found it on the way back of the tub. I felt something touching my legs as I tried to sleep and woke up to blankets tucked in around me…weeeeee it was a blast to say the least!

***

Monday, November 07, 2005 11:41 A.M.
u better not be there
We were there in August. just a couple of weeks before Katrina. I am hoping Creole Gardens faired OK and everyone associated with it.

My paranormal group wants to come down this next summer to do an investigation, so I have emailed Uly about it.

Visit The Creole's website and see what new experiences have occurred since the writing of this book.

CHAPTER 18
The Whaley House

Located in historic Old Town San Diego
at 2476 San Diego Avenue, San Diego, CA 92110

GHOSTLY LEGENDS OF THE WHALEY HOUSE

Located in historic Old Town San Diego, the "birthplace of California," the Whaley House stands today as a classic example of mid-nineteenth century Greek Revival architecture. Formally dedicated as a historic house museum on May 25, 1960, and open to the public ever since, it is one of San Diego's most popular visitor destinations. Over 100,000 people visit the Whaley House annually, with guests traveling from across the globe to experience this world-renowned museum.

Few houses in San Diego are as historically important as the Whaley House. In addition to being the Whaley family home, it housed a granary, the County Court House, San Diego's first commercial theater, various businesses including Thomas Whaley's own general store, a ballroom, a billiard hall, school, and polling place.

Significant events, such as the seizure of the court documents and records in 1871, and the suicide of Violet Whaley in 1885 profoundly affected Thomas and Anna Whaley. These events, as well as the hangings which occurred on the property before the house was constructed, have suffused the Whaley House with an air of mystery and added to its reputation as something more than just California State Historic Landmark #65.

The Whaley Family History

Thomas Whaley came to California in 1849 during the Gold Rush. He set up a store with George Wardle on Montgomery Street where he sold hardware and woodwork from his family's New York business and offered mining equipment and utensils on consignment. This young entrepreneur's great-grandfather, Alexander Whaley, participated in the Boston Tea Party and the Revolutionary War where he provided flintlock muskets for soldiers and the use of his house on Long Island by General George Washington

He returned to New York to marry his sweetheart, Anna Eloise DeLaunay, on May 14, 1853.

By 1858, Thomas and Anna Whaley had produced three children: Francis, Thomas (who died at just 18 months), and Anna Amelia. In August 1858, an arson-set fire destroyed Whaley's business on the Plaza. Despondent over this loss and the death of Thomas earlier that year, the family moved to San Francisco.

In San Francisco, Whaley worked as an U.S. Army Commissary Storekeeper. Three more children, George, Violet, and Corinne, were born. After a major earthquake in May 1868, the Whaley couple and their five children returned to the brick house in San Diego, out of which Whaley & Crosthwaite ran a general store.

On January 5, 1882, Violet Whaley and Anna Amelia Whaley married in Old San Diego, probably in this house. Anna married her first cousin, John T. Whaley, and Violet wed George T. Bertolacci, which proved unbearable. After a divorce, which caused Violet tremendous humiliation in 1884 and a period of great depression monitored by the local physician, she committed suicide at the home by shooting herself through the heart on August 18, 1885.

Anna, Thomas' widow, Lillian (Corinne), then assistant at the Public Library, Francis, and George, a musician all lived in the old dwelling in 1912. On February 24, 1913, Anna died in the house. Francis passed away in the home on November 19, 1914. Lillian continued residency in the structure until her death in 1953. Because she had spent the better part of the first half of the twentieth century in the house alone, it had fallen once again into a terrible state of disrepair.

Hauntings...

According to the Travel Channel's *America's Most Haunted*, the house is the number one most haunted house in the United States.

The alleged hauntings of the Whaley House have been reported on numerous other television programs and been written up in countless publications and books since the house first opened as a museum in 1960. Although we cannot state positively that the Whaley House is really haunted, the voluminous documentation of paranormal occurrences at the site makes a compelling case. But, if there are ghosts at the Whaley House, who are they and why are they here?

Yankee Jim

The earliest documented ghost at the Whaley House is "Yankee Jim." James (aka Santiago) Robinson was convicted of attempted grand larceny in San Diego in 1852 and hanged on a gallows off the back of a wagon on the site where the house now stands.

The local newspaper reported that he "kept his feet in the wagon as long as possible, but was finally pulled off. He swung back and forth like a pendulum until he strangled to death." Although Thomas Whaley had been a spectator at the execution, he did not let it dissuade him from buying the property a few years later and building a home for his family there.

According to the *San Diego Union*, "Soon after the couple and their children moved in, heavy footsteps were heard moving about the house. Whaley described them as sounding as though they were made by the boots of a large man. Finally he came to the conclusion that these unexplained footfalls were made by Yankee Jim Robinson."

Another source states that Lillian Whaley, the Whaley's youngest daughter, who lived in the house until 1953, "had been convinced the ghost of "Yankee Jim" haunted the Old House."

Other Ghostly Encounters

A visitor to the museum in 1962 mentioned, "The ghost had driven her family from their visit there more than 60 years earlier. Her mother was unnerved by the phantom walking noise and the strange way the windows unlatched and flew up."

Many visitors to the house have reported encountering Thomas Whaley himself. The late June Reading, former curator of the museum, said, "We had a little girl perhaps five or six years old who waved to a man she said was standing in the parlor. We couldn't see him. But often children's sensitivity is greater than an adult's." However, many adults have reported seeing the apparition of Mr. Whaley, usually on the upper landing. One said he was "clad in frock coat and pantaloons, the face turned away from her, so she could not make it out. Suddenly it faded away."

The specter of Anna Whaley has also been reported, usually in the downstairs rooms or in the garden. In 1964, Mrs. Whaley's floating, drifting spirit appeared to television personality Regis Philbin. Philbin said that all of a sudden he noticed something on the wall...filmy white ...and that it looked like an apparition of some kind. He got so excited that he flipped on the flashlight and nothing there was there except a portrait of Anna Whaley, the long-dead mistress of the house.

Other visitors have described seeing or sensing the presence of a woman in the courtroom. "I see a small figure of a woman," one visitor said, "who has a swarthy complexion. She is wearing a long full skirt, reaching to the floor. The skirt appears to be a calico or gingham, small print. She has a kind of cap on her head, dark hair, and eyes and she is wearing gold hoops in her pierced ears. She seems to stay in this room, lives here, I gather." None of the Whaleys fit this description, but the house was rented out to numerous tenants over the years. Perhaps the mysterious woman in the courtroom was one of these.

Another presence reported by visitors and docents is that of a young girl, who is usually found in the dining room.

Psychic Sybil Leek encountered this spirit during a visit in the 1960s. She said that it was a long-haired girl, very quick, and in a longish dress. She went to the table in a room and Sybil went to the chair.

Urban legend has it that this is the ghost of a playmate of the Whaley children. She accidentally broke her neck on a low-hanging clothesline in the backyard, and whose name was either Annabel or Carrie Washburn. There are no historic records of any child dying this way at the Whaley House; nor is there record of any family named Washburn residing in San Diego at the time. It is believed that the legend was started by a one-time employee of the Whaley House, in an effort to add to the house's mystique.

Even animals aren't left out of the singular occurrences. A parapsychologist reported he saw a spotted dog, like a fox terrier, that ran down the hall with his ears flapping and into the dining room. The dog, he said, was an apparition. When they lived in the house, the Whaley's owned a terrier named Dolly Varden.

The Whaley House stands silently watching over San Diego Avenue as it has done for a century and a half. Every day visitors come from around the world to tour the historic museum. It contains so much history within its walls, that even the non-believer will enjoy the tour.

The Whaley House has been structurally altered several times in its 150 years of existence. Finally, in the late 1950s after the county purchased the property, many changes were made to prepare the building to function as a museum. The original lean-to kitchen was demolished, as was the latter-day bathroom and a doorway was added to the wall dividing the courtroom and the general store. The roof was replaced, a back window was changed to a door; a new flight of stairs was added to the back of the house, and inside courses of bricks were removed from the outer walls (and used for patching), and replaced with steel and concrete.

For believers and skeptics alike, the house draws them back time and again, in search of those elusive ghosts.

THE END?

Lightning Source UK Ltd.
Milton Keynes UK
UKOW051112020112

184625UK00001B/44/P